Tunisia's Global Integration

A Second Generation of Reforms to Boost Growth and Employment

THE WORLD BANK
Washington, D.C.

World Bank Country Studies are among the many reports originally prepared for internal use as part of the continuing analysis by the Bank of the economic and related conditions of its developing member countries and to facilitate its dialogs with the governments. Some of the reports are published in this series with the least possible delay for the use of governments, and the academic, business, financial, and development communities. The manuscript of this paper therefore has not been prepared in accordance with the procedures appropriate to formally-edited texts. Some sources cited in this paper may be informal documents that are not readily available.

ISBN-13: 978-0-8213-7668-3
eISBN: 978-0-8213-7711-6
ISSN: 0253-2123   DOI: 10.1596/978-0-8213-7668-3

Library of Congress Cataloging-in-Publication Data has been requested.

Contents

LIST OF TABLES

LIST OF FIGURES

LIST OF BOXES

Preface

Tunisia's past integration policies have led to a significant increase in FDI flows to the country, and to a rise of textiles and clothing and of automobile electrical and mechanical components exports through participation to EU production networks. Economic sectors highly integrated to the global market have been able to attract investment, converge to EU's labor productivity standards, and boost job creation. These trends helped Tunisia's sustain an average 5 percent growth over the last 20 years. This performance places Tunisia among the best performers in the region and in emerging countries.

Today Tunisia is entering a new phase in its integration process and the impressive results achieved so far, important challenges remain: (i) FDI increases are not accompanied by a rapid increase in domestic investment, which remains sluggish; (ii) in spite of reforms in recent years, the business climate for import-competing and non-tradable sectors can be further improved and, perhaps more importantly; (iii) trade integration has largely bypassed non-tourism service sectors and the structural transformation of the service sector is relatively slow. Addressing these challenges will be crucial to meet the 11th Plan's growth target of 6.1 percent over 2007–11 and to reduce unemployment, which stands at 14 percent.

The government has asked the Bank to (i) examine the key integration challenges that the country's manufacturing sector is facing at the end of 10 years of tariff dismantling vis-à-vis the EU, (ii) suggest the key remaining reforms needed to further enhance the competitive position of the country in the Euro-med space, and (iii) identify the specific reforms needed to realize the largely untapped potential in services.[1]

This report addresses these issues. Chapter 1 takes stock of the integration policies implemented since the early 1970s and assessed their impact on FDI, exports and employment. Chapter 2 looks at today's major challenges in the manufacturing sector and the specific policies needed to address them. Chapter 3 assesses the entry, business, and trade restrictions in Tunisia's key backbone services sectors (telecommunication, banking, air transport, accounting, auditing, and legal services) using a well-focused regulatory questionnaire. The restrictiveness indices calculated from the regulatory questionnaire are then used to benchmark Tunisia against OECD and some emerging economies and to simulate the impact of various liberalization options on the price of services and the economy via a multi-region general equilibrium model. Finally, chapter 4 examines the prospect for increasing exports and off shoring of a large number of services for which Tunisia has demonstrated a strong capacity for export in recent years.

This report was prepared by a core team led by Ndiamé Diop and composed of Olivier Cattaneo, Philippa Dee, Sun Young Lee, Mariem Malouche, Gallina A. Vincellette, and Peter Walkenhorst. Chapter 1 was written by Ndiamé Diop and Gallina A. Vincelette, Chapter 2 by Ndiamé Diop and Mariem Malouche, Chapter 3 by Ndiamé Diop and Philippa Dee, and

---

1. The opportunity of including agriculture in the present study has been largely discussed with the government at the concept note stage. It was decided to leave it out, because an analysis of integration issues in agriculture was completed by the Bank in 2006 ("Tunisia Agricultural Policy Review").

Chapter 4 by Peter Walkenhorst and Olivier Cattaneo. The report builds on several background notes and contributions from Magueye Dia (note on financial sector), Philippa Dee (background paper on services modeling), Bartek Kaminski (note on air transport), and Carlo M. Rossotto and Anat Lewin (background report on telecom).

The report benefited from helpful comments from the peer reviewers, Richard Newfarmer, Mona Haddad, and Marouane El Abassi. Valuable comments were also received from Hedi Larbi, Bernard Hoekman, Farrukh Iqbal, Cecile Fruman, Carlos Silva-Jauregui, Omer M. Karasapan, Najy Benhassine, Hamid Alavi, Vincent Palmade, John Panzer, Dominique Van Der Mensbrugghe, and Paul Brenton. Contributions were also received from Irina Shaorshadze, Narjes Jerbi, Chaitri Hapugalle, and Daniela Marotta.

Miria A. Pigato supervised the team and provided excellent guidance and support throughout; the team thanks Mustapha K. Nabli and Theodore H. Ahlers for their key strategic guidance, comments, encouragements and support throughout.

Finally, the report could not be completed without the very productive collaboration and excellent inputs and contributions from the Ministry of Development and International Cooperation (MDCI). We collaborated closely with *Institut d'Economie Quantitative (IEQ)* in particular, and wish to thank the IEQ economists and their former Director General Mr. Abdelhamid Triki. The team is also grateful to the Tunisian authorities in other Ministries who helped with various aspects of the study and provided valuable inputs in the discussion of the study. The contribution of the various firms and persons met during the preparation of this study in Tunis is also acknowledged.

The report was formatted by Khalid Alouane with important contributions from Narjes Jerbi and Angela Hawkins. Nicole W. De Blaye assured the translation of the report into French.

The team thanks the Multi-donor trade trust fund (MDTTF) for its generous financial support of our Bank work on trade in Tunisia.

Introduction and Summary

Tunisia's Real Income Growth Has Been Remarkable

In 1961, Tunisia's GDP per capita (in purchasing power parity, PPP) was lower than Turkey's but higher than Malaysia's and Thailand's, two East Asian countries that share many similarities with Tunisia.[2] In 2006, it reached $6859 (in PPP), the second highest in the Maghreb (after oil-rich Libya's) and on par with Turkey's. However, Tunisia's impressive performance falls short of that of Malaysia whose GDP per capita is now 30 percent higher.

The significant increase in real incomes in Tunisia is the result of solid GDP growth since the mid-1960s (5 percent a year), low inflation and the demographic transition, faster than in neighboring countries.[3] Since 1996, economic growth has exhibited greater resilience to moderate exogenous shocks, thanks to prudent macroeconomic management.[4] Public debt, while still high, declined from 62.4 percent in 2001 to 50.9 percent of GDP in 2007 thanks to pro-active debt management (Figure 2). The resulting decline in the debt service in recent years combined with steady GDP growth allowed the government to "protect" capital expenditures and key social spending within the context of low but structural fiscal deficit (Figure 3). While the current account remained in deficit over the last 10 years (−2.9 on average), foreign exchange reserves increased steadily thanks to increasing FDI inflows. In 2007, international reserves increased by US$ 1 billion to US$ 7.8 billion, representing 4.6 months of imports of goods and services.

---

2. As discussed below, one key similarity between these countries is their early reliance on trade integration and FDI to fuel growth.

3. Tunisia's fertility rate, at 7 children per woman in 1961, started to decline in 1967—after a new family code changed the conditions of marriage and guaranteed women's rights—to reach 2.04 in 2005.

4. For instance, GDP grew by 4.2 percent in 2005 despite a 5 percent decline in agriculture.

1

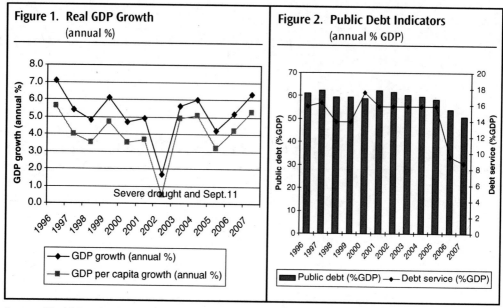

Source: World Development Indicators and Ministry of Finance, Tunisia.

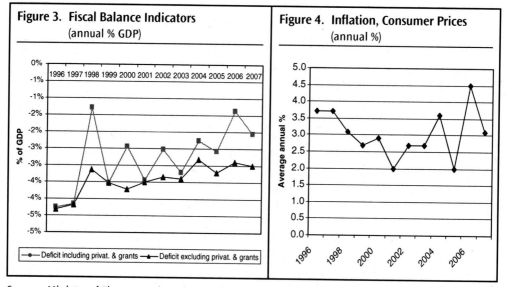

Source: Ministry of Finance and Institut National Statistique, Tunisia.

Aggregate growth accounting reveals that GDP growth reflected productivity growth more than capital deepening. Total factor productivity (TFP) explained about 43.4 percent of GDP growth since the mid-1960s, while traditional factors altogether contributed about 56.6 percent of the per capita growth in that period (Figure 5). The important contribution of productivity reflects the country's steady investment in education and health since the early 1960s and strong achievements in human capital development.[5] But beyond this factor, productivity growth reflects the rapid development of an offshore sector largely integrated with EU production networks as well as more recent opening of the industrial sector to competition as part of the Tunisia-EU Association Agreement (AA) as discussed below.

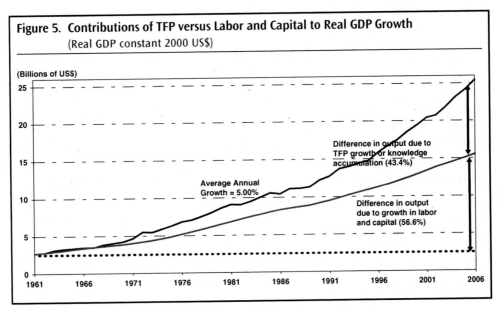

Figure 5. Contributions of TFP versus Labor and Capital to Real GDP Growth
(Real GDP constant 2000 US$)

Source: World Bank WBI's Knowledge Assessment data

Trade Integration Has Played a Key Role

Throughout the 1960s, Tunisia maintained a strict import-substitution policy: nominal and effective protection rates were very high and almost all imports required some kind of licensing and/or administrative approval (Nabli and others 1999). The heavy anti-export bias inherent in the restrictive import regime strongly hindered exports, which were heavily dominated by fuel (more than 50 percent of exports). To prevent restrictions in trade and domestic markets from spilling over to the export sector, the government created an "offshore" sector in 1972 and put in place generous fiscal and financial incentives to attract foreign direct investments (FDI) and boost exports. Wholly exporting firms were given an "enclave" business environment, with duty-free raw material and equipment imports, 10-year corporate tax holiday, free repatriation of profits and trade facilitation services (for example, "in-house" customs clearance). In the Mid-1990s, the government began to unravel its heterogeneous trade policy stance and started to dismantle tariffs on EU industrial products in order to form a free trade area with its largest economic partner by 2008. Effective integration with Europe led to an important decline in tariffs faced by EU. Tariffs on EU industrial goods dropped from about 100 percent in 1996 to about 4 percent in 2007.

---

5. Tunisia has near universal primary enrollment and one of the highest university enrollment rates in the Middle East and North Africa Region (33 percent, with women representing 57 percent of students). The number of engineers, technicians, accountants, and doctors per capita is one of the highest in the region.

The government accompanied the opening of the industrial sector with the implementation of an upgrading (*mise a niveau and industrial modernization*) program, aimed at enhancing the organizational, technological, and marketing capabilities of firms being gradually exposed to competition vis-à-vis the EU. Further, much effort was deployed to facilitate global integration through trade facilitation measures. Electronic documentation processing was introduced (Tunisia Trade Net), but also streamlined technical controls, improved customs procedures, and increased access to information on standards and technical regulations to raise transparency and meet international trade obligations.

The above policies literally transformed the economy. Thanks to a dramatic increase in FDI, export of textiles and clothing increased dramatically and led to a diversification of exports away from fuel. The share of fuel exports plummeted from 52 percent to 13 percent between 1980 and 2006, giving way to textiles and clothing whose share increased from 18 to 33 percent. Since 1997, increased participation in EU automobile production networks (France, Italy, and Germany mainly) has led to double-digit growth rates of exports of engineering and electrical components and a second wave of structural transformation. The share of "mechanical and electrical engineering" products in total exports increased from 9.5 percent in 1995 to around 19 percent in 2006. Tunisia is now of Europe's top 10 suppliers of automobile electrical wiring systems and the country's global market share in this segment is about 2.2 percent.

The impact of global integration on employment has been positive. To illustrate, in 1980, 8 years after its creation, the offshore sector employed about 10,000 people; in 1990, total employment in this sector reached 70,000 workers and; today, with more than 245,000 persons working under that regime, the offshore sector represents 54 percent of total manufacturing jobs and 8 percent of all jobs in the country. Furthermore, the increasing development of mechanical and electrical engineering is leading to an interesting gradual movement toward more skill and technology-intensive specialization that could help absorb unemployed university graduates.

Important Challenges Remain However

While quite decent, Tunisia's past growth (4.5 percent in the 10th development plan-2002–2006) is insufficient to reduce unemployment significantly. Indeed, the unemployment rate remains high at 14 percent. Unemployment is particularly high among women (16 percent), individuals between ages 25 and 29 (20 percent), and individuals below age 25 (30 percent). A recent tracer study showed that more than 45 percent of higher education graduates from the 2004 cohort were unemployed 18 months after receiving their diploma (World Bank 2007).

In the country's 11th Development Plan (2007–11), an annual growth of 6.1 percent is deemed necessary to achieve the government's employment objectives. According to the government's calculations, this would require a significant increase in investment and exports, assuming that private consumption will maintain its current contribution to real GDP growth (64 percent). Precisely, investment (including FDI) would need to increase significantly from 23 percent of GDP currently to 25.3 percent by 2011. Second, trade needs to play an even greater role than in the past, as exports and imports should increase annually by 7 and 6 percent respectively.

Clearly, further increasing investment, export and productivity growth require continuing reforms in the areas of skills development, financial sector, investment climate and infrastructure development. This study shows that global integration should also play a central role. As shown in Figure 6, global integration has been a crucial tool to enhance productivity and growth. Tunisia's labor productivity in the manufacturing sectors exposed to international competition is catching up with the EU, standing at 73 percent of EU's (a 27 percent gap). In sharp contrast, the average productivity is only 33 percent of EU's (67 percent gap) in the least globally exposed manufacturing sectors. In the not-so-open services sector, labor productivity is about 45 percent of EU's. Clearly, a large potential of productivity gain exist in the onshore manufacturing and the services sectors.

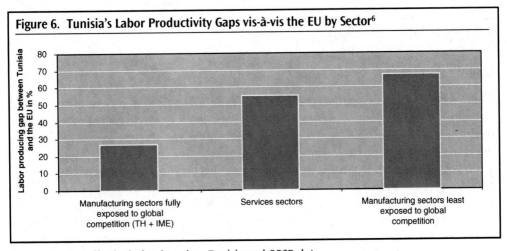

Figure 6. Tunisia's Labor Productivity Gaps vis-à-vis the EU by Sector[6]

Source: Bank staff calculation based on Tunisia and OECD data.

What Integration Reforms?

Moving to a "Global" Integration Approach

Tunisia has so far opted for integrating with the world economy in a "preferential" fashion. Indeed, the country has opened up vis-à-vis preferential partners (the EU, GAFTA and other preferential partners) and maintained high protection vis-à-vis non-preferential partners. For instance, while the average tariff faced by EU industrial products is now zero, the one faced by non-preferential partners (the applied, misnamed, "most-favored nation" (MFN) tariff) is about 24 percent.[7] Tunisia now faces a dilemma: maintaining the current large gap between preferential and the MFN tariffs may fuel fraud and parallel markets and further reduce investment by formal firms. On the other hand, reducing the gap abruptly may hurt production and jobs (China has lower prices than

---

6. Sectors exposed to international trade are textiles and clothing and mechanical and electrical engineering. The other manufacturing sectors are considered as less exposed to international trade.

7. EU agro-processing products still face non-zero tariffs, so the average zero concern non-agro-processing industrial products.

the EU). Unfortunately, Tunisia has today reached a point where further reductions of tariffs on imports from the EU without reducing tariffs on other import sources would reduce welfare because of trade diversion. In other words, the cost of trade diversion now outweighs the welfare benefit of further tariff reductions on EU imports of industrial goods, which suggests that a decisive move toward reducing the MFN tariff rates is needed in the near future.

Simulations conducted in this report using GTAP modeling show that the adjustment pressures in manufacturing from a reduction of MFN tariffs by 25 percent would not be large, because the initial levels of applied tariffs on industrial goods are not as important as in agriculture. The worst affected sectors—wood and paper products, metals and products, and transport equipment—would be smaller than otherwise by 10 percent or less after about ten years as a result of eliminating the remaining tariffs on EU imports and cutting tariffs on imports from other sources by 25 percent.[8] Furthermore, the impact on consumers and exports would be positive. Exports would increase by 27 percent as a result of a 25 percent cut in MFN tariffs.

Making the Onshore Sector More Competitive

Another by-product of past integration policies that reduces efficiency in the economy is that, with the increasing openness of the onshore sector to international competition, the former anti-export bias in trade policy is vanishing and the incentive gap between offshore and onshore sectors is turning discriminatory.

In fact, the government has been gradually reducing the incentive gap between onshore and offshore sectors in recent years. For instance, (i) tariffs on raw materials, equipment and capital goods are now reduced to zero for onshore firms in many sectors, whether the imports originate from a preferential partner or not; (ii) export promotion tools are reaching more and more onshore firms (for example, FAMEX), helping reduce market access disadvantage of the latter; (iii) on December 2006, a fiscal law reduced the onshore corporate tax from 35 to 30 percent, increased VAT reimbursement to 100 percent as of 2008, re-balanced VAT rates (6, 12 and 18 percent) and suppressed the 29 percent rate and (iv) finally, offshore firms are now allowed to sell up to 30 percent of their production in the onshore sector and be subject to the onshore fiscal regime on that proportion.

Still, in contrast with offshore firms, formal enterprises selling in the domestic market suffer from anti-competitive practices and unfair competition stemming from informality, tax and social security avoidance, etc. and face more difficulties in the credit and labor markets. In a recent Enterprise Survey, about 60 percent of firms operating in the domestic market denounced anti-competitive practices such as implicit agreements, discrimination among clients and linked sales (IEQ 2006b). Regarding unfair competition, 67 percent of firms denounced at least one type of unfair competition in the domestic market. While Tunisia's competition laws are up to international standards, implementation issues remain and the capacities of the competition authorities could be enhanced. Constraints in the credit and labor markets are long standing issues. Reforms in the credit market are well underway but reforms aimed at making the firing laws less rigid will be needed.

---

8. Given the standard limitations of CGE modeling however, a careful and more detailed analysis of the impact of tariff reform is necessary to anticipate possible difficulties and devise offsetting/compensating measures.

Furthermore, Tunisia's manufacturing sector faces particular challenges emanating from heightened competition with reforming countries within the region. First, Tunisia's competitors in the region are catching up fast in terms of attracting foreign direct investments. While Tunisia is still ahead in terms of share of FDI in GDP, FDI inflows are increasing much faster in Morocco, Egypt and Turkey; second, while Tunisia enjoys low factor costs (labor, energy, land, and so forth) and moderate transport costs, logistics services and constraints should be addressed to enhance connectivity with the global market and attract new investments; finally, while the country has a solid performance in terms of investment in innovation "inputs," further improvement in innovation and technological absorption is necessary.

Harnessing the Potential in Services Sectors

Although addressing the priority integration issues in the goods sector is likely to contribute to growth in the long run, the bulk of productivity (thus competitiveness) gains and economic expansion in the years ahead will occur in services. The services sector is now Tunisia's most dynamic sector in terms of value-added, with an average annual growth rate of 7 percent over the last 10 years. Still, the country is far from exploiting the sector's large potential. The share of commercial services in GDP, at 47 percent, is lower than for the lower-tier of OECD countries and emerging economies. Further, 80 percent of Tunisia's services export revenues come from tourism, travel, and transport services. Tunisia's well-educated labor force and its convenient location next to the EU make it a very strong potential contender in the many service markets.

Liberalizing Backbone Services. The *Institut d'Economie Quantitative's* recent report on competitiveness shows that just over half of Tunisian firms consider the cost of credit a major constraint, while about one-fifth of them rate telecom services as costly (telephone) and of inadequate availability and quality (Internet). The cost of transport services, mainly air transport, is also a major constraint.

Greater openness of backbone services to trade and investment could reduce these constraints, as the experience of some segments of the telecom sector (mobile) has shown. Tunisia has undertaken a gradual opening of backbone services sectors to private competition but many entry barriers hinder entry into services sectors. The country has today no free trade agreement (FTA) that includes services. Multilateral liberalization of services under WTO's GATS has been very limited with only three sectors (tourism, telecom and financial sectors) included in the GATS Uruguay Round (UR). While some of the sectors not included are quite open (for example maritime transport), entry into many services sectors is restricted. For instance, all trading activities, including wholesale distribution and retail trading services, are reserved for enterprises in which Tunisians hold a majority interest. For some services activities, foreign investment requires the prior agreement of the *Commission Supérieure des Investissements* (CSI—Investment Commission) if the foreign participation exceeds 50 percent of the company capital (for example, in insurance). Finally, the measures affecting the presence of natural persons (Mode 4) remain unbound, with the exception of wholly exporting enterprises that can recruit up to four executives and managers of foreign nationality.

Beside ongoing trade negotiations under GATS Doha round, Tunisia has started a process of negotiations for a services trade agreement with the EU in March 2006 under the Euro-med context. Discussions of the general provisions of the agreements have started. These will be followed by bilateral negotiations on market access commitments (which services are to be included and what degree of openness). The EU has proposed putting the future agreements in the context of the European Neighborhood Policy and to use some of the implementation tools of this initiative, chiefly regulatory convergence, in some sectors. For Tunisia, mode 4 (temporary movement of professional services providers) and mode 2 in the area of health services represent two big areas of interest. These negotiations are crucial to secure better market access for its services providers to Europe, which would require a relaxing of restrictions in obtaining visas and mutual recognition agreements for diplomas and professional qualifications with some EU countries. Tunisia is less interested in mode 3 (commercial presence) given its limited number of multinationals and in mode 1 (consumption abroad) given the prevalence of capital controls.

The detailed sector-by-sector analysis of regulatory barriers and their impacts undertaken in this study shows that greater openness of backbone services can reduce prices and increase productivity through increased FDI, vertical knowledge spillovers, and market expansion. Liberalizing these sectors would also improve the ability of Tunisian firms to export goods and services, through secondary effects. For instance, the ability to participate in business process outsourcing and to export ICT-enabled services (such as call centers) depends on the state of telecom services. However, opening reform should be accompanied by a strengthening of regulation and oversight. The typical reform agenda would include private participation, market contestability and competition, and regulatory oversight improvement.

Boosting the Exports of Emerging Services: Professional Services and ICTs. A promising area for offshoring is Tunisia's emerging services. Driven by considerable reductions in communications, transport, and transaction costs, trade in commercial services has grown considerably. Within the global services sector, professional and ICT-enabled services, for which Tunisia has demonstrated a real capacity for export in recent years, are among the most dynamic growth segments.[9] One development fueling the growth of exports of professional and ICT-enabled services is that firms in high-income countries outsource back office and information technology functions to take advantage of advanced skills and lower labor costs of specialized service providers.

Outsourcing from the French market is projected to grow at an annual rate of 12–13 percent over the next five years. Tunisia's wage advantage over Europe is not as pronounced as that of competitors in East Asia, but its geographical and cultural proximity, its established commercial ties, and its strong French-speaking communities make it the destination of choice for "near-shoring" by French and other francophone companies. But Morocco and Eastern European countries are serious contenders in this market. Chapter 4 outlines some key reforms needed if Tunisia is to succeed. They include reducing of restrictions to market access in professional services, encouraging of structural consolidation to gain economies of scale, further reform in telecom services, and providing specific training in some areas.

---

9. Rapid advances in information and communication technologies and the ongoing global liberalization of trade and investment in services have increased the tradability of these service activities and enabled the production of services to be increasingly location-independent (OECD, 2006).

Recommendation Matrix

Issue	Recommendations	Reform Anchor/Actors
Policy Issues in the goods sector		
Tariff policy:		
Large gaps between tariffs faced by "preferential" and "non preferential (or Most-Favored Nation)" partners	- Reduce MFN tariffs by at least 25% in the short run to avoid trade diversion and growth of parallel markets; - Reduce to zero tariffs on raw material imported from "non preferential" partners to enhance competitiveness of all firms; - Seek to come up with an average NPF tariff of 10–15% in the medium term	Unilateral reform
Narrow focus of existing Free Trade Agreements	- Discuss negative lists with partners in view of revising them downward and making them consistent across FTAs; - Deepen trade agreements to include/ implement reciprocal liberalization in services, including regionally	Bilateral and pluri-lateral
Cumbersome Free Trade Agreements	- Harmonize overlapping provisions between GAFTA and bilateral agreements; - Negotiate in any new Free Trade Agreement "third party" rules of origin to maximize the impact of the agreement	Regional (GAFTA) technical committee discussion then introduction of amendments at Ministerial meetings; Bilateral and pluri-lateral negotiations
Dichotomy offshore– onshore sector:		
Anti-competitive practices in the domestic market	- Better advertise the new competition legislation; - Further increase the capacities of the competition authorities (more human and materiel resources);	Unilateral reform
Rigidity in the labor market	- Reduce the rigidity in firing laws and provide more protection outside firms; - Increase the flexibility in the rules and procedures governing retrenchments to facilitate firm restructuring	Unilateral reform
Difficult access to credit by onshore firms	- Pursue ongoing reforms aimed at reducing non-performing loans and promoting the creation of well-regulated private credit registries; - Reform the SICAR to make them more effective in accompanying investors without collaterals (especially young university graduates)	Unilateral reform

(continued)

Recommendation Matrix (*Continued*)		
Issue	**Recommendations**	**Reform Anchor/Actors**
Competitive positioning in the Euro-Med:		
Poor and fragmented logistics services	Reduce entry barriers in the logistics sector: - Simplify the "cahier des charges" to strictly assure quality standards; - Allow foreign majority ownership participation - Encourage investment in modern warehouses and logistics platforms; - Deepen trade facilitation at the ports (more automation, more streamlining of procedures, and greater involvement of private operators)	Unilateral reform
Direct connection with Asia and the USA	- Pursue investment in deep water port (e.g., Enfidha)	Unilateral/PPP
Technological development and innovation	- Pro-actively promote partnership between Tunisia's innovation institutions and European ones; - Further strengthen firm-university collaboration and collaboration within existing technopoles; - Promote ICT diffusion targeting small firms (see also reforms of telecom); - Reduce bureaucracy in the innovation system	Bilateral cooperation (e.g., institutional twinning with the EU) Unilateral reform
Reforms of backbone services		
Telecommunication:		
Lack of competition in fixed telephony	- Award new licenses to boost private investment and competition in this segment to reduce prices and improve services;	Unilateral reform
Duopolistic mobile telephony market	- Allow entry of a new 2G/3G operator in the market to further boost competition to the benefit of consumers and firm - Promote competition among providers of 3rd generation mobile services	Unilateral reform
Quality of regulation in telecom	- Enhance the policing and inspection power of the INT; - Mandate the INT to be involved in litigations related to anti-competitive practices; - Encourage the collaboration between the INT and the "Conseil de Concurrence" on telecom and IT matters;	Unilateral reform

(*continued*)

Recommendation Matrix (*Continued*)

Issue	Recommendations	Reform Anchor/Actors
	- Introduce in Tunisia's legislation the concept of technologically-neutral licenses and class licenses - Assess regulatory gap with the EU and decide on a convergence plan as part of the EU-Tunisia Neighborhood Partnership	
Banking:		
Difficulties faced by foreign banks in lending and raising funds domestically	- Lift the restrictions in the regulations	Unilateral/Bind under Doha GATS
Foreign majority ownership limit	- Allow foreign majority ownership in banking	Unilateral/Bind under Doha GATS
Fragmentation in legal texts governing credits	- Update the 1987 legislation (outdated) and consolidate the numerous executive orders and "circulaires"	Unilateral reform
Quality of regulation in Banking	- Gradually adopt Basel II and IFRS/IAS standards; - Assess regulatory gap with the EU and decide on a convergence plan as part of the EU-Tunisia Neighborhood Partnership	Unilateral reform
Foreign exchange controls (mode 1 transactions)	- Gradual removal conditioned on the regulatory and institutional strengthening of the sector (the current government plan)	Unilateral reform
Air Transport Services		
Integration with the EU	- Negotiate a horizontal agreement to replace old bilateral agreements with the EU Members following the EU's adoption of a single skies with its member countries (short run);	Bilateral agreement
	- Consider accepting EU's offer of an "open skies" agreement to further reduce airfare and upgrade Tunisia's smaller airports (with EU support)	Bilateral agreement
Professional services (engineering, accounting, auditing and legal services)		
Access to EU market under Mode 4	- Seek a mutual recognition agreement of diplomas, professional qualification and certification with France and other EU countries;	Bilateral agreement

(continued)

Recommendation Matrix (*Continued*)		
Issue	**Recommendations**	**Reform Anchor/Actors**
	- Seek a specific agreement with France allowing Tunisian service providers a more systematic access (currently, a decision by the Ministry of Finance and Foreign Affairs is needed (France's national treatment and market access regulations for independent providers under GATS under mode 4 remain unbound))	Bilateral agreement
	- Support professional organization seeking arrangement with specific European Embassies for a more systematic granting of visas (provide guarantees)	Team-up with professional organizations
Regional trade in professional services	- Seek a mutual recognition agreement of diplomas, professional qualification and certification with the Maghreb and Mena countries - Sign agreement of free establishment of professional services (investment) within the region—harmonize licensing procedures and standards/rules - Multiply at the regional level agreements on social security and health expense reimbursement with private insurance companies of the region; - Negotiate double taxation treaties with regional partners	Bilateral agreements
Access to the Tunisian market	- Unilaterally relax the requirement in law and accounting for partners of local firms to be local and require partners to be simply locally licensed to promote outsourcing (exploit mode 3 and mode 1 complementarities);	Unilateral reform
	- Consider removing the nationality requirement for entry into the medical, accounting, legal and engineering services markets (to be consistent with the policy of seeking mutual recognition);	Unilateral
Boosting Exports of emerging services		
Improve Statistics on services	- Disaggregate the category "services to firms" in the balance of payment statistics - Submit yearly questionnaire to services exporters to collect information on services exported through the temporary movement of professionals	

(*continued*)

Recommendation Matrix (*Continued*)

Issue	Recommendations	Reform Anchor/Actors
	- Report exports of health services not wholly under "travel" in the balance of payment but disaggregate; - Capture the number of foreign patients using health facilities in Tunisia and the related expenditures on health	
Formulate an Export strategy	- Create an inter-ministerial committee for export of new services strategy; - Design a 5-year strategic plan for export of health services	Unilateral reform
Restrictions to market entry and operation	- To boost mode 1 (off-shoring) and mode 2 (domestic consumption) exports, allow mode 3 FDI (complementarities between mode 1 and mode 3) in the health, accounting and legal (see also above) - Assess the corpus of rules governing business in the health sector (medical tourism needs to be better regulated) and the respect of medical deontology and good practices - Clarify the regulation and procedures for authorizing the opening of a private hospital	Unilateral reform/ Bilateral negotiation with the EU
Quality of labor and professional standards in health, accounting, legal and legal services	Adjust training (including vocational training) to meet private sector demand; - In health, improve the training of nurses and medical support staff; - In engineering, include new disciplines such as communication and marketing - In legal studies, internationalize the curriculum (international standards); - For all professional services, enhance language skills, in particular French and English;	Unilateral reform
Constraints related to public tenders	Streamline tendering practices and adopt more timely payment schedules	Unilateral reform

CHAPTER 1

Tunisia's Integration Policies and Their Impacts

This chapter examines Tunisia's key integration policies and assesses their impacts on FDI, export and employment. The main findings are as follows:

- From the early 1970s to the mid-1990s, Tunisia implemented a heterodox policy stance, featuring a heavy protection of the domestic industries and generous FDI and export promotion incentives to offset the anti-export bias generated by protection. Since the mid-1990s, external trade is being gradually liberalized, while trade facilitation policies have gained prominence. The openness of the industrial sector is largely driven by the association agreement with the EU, Tunisia's leading economic partner with which it will form a free trade area in industrial goods as of January 2008;

- The impact of the policies implemented on FDI, exports and employment has been dramatic. Initial FDI flows to the textiles and clothing industry led to a first wave of structural transformation away from fuel export toward light manufacturing (textiles and clothing), with a robust impact on exports, productivity growth and employment. Furthermore, in spite of a dramatic drop in tariffs on imports originating from the EU (from 100 percent in 1996 to 4 percent in 2007), many import-substitute industries have adjusted well and have avoided stagnation/decline in spite of mounting difficulties;

- Today, Tunisia is slowly embarking in a second wave of structural transformation, featuring greater participation to the EU automobile industry networks. The share of mechanical and electrical parts and components in total export is increasing rapidly, leading to an interesting gradual movement toward more skill and technology-intensive specialization that could help absorb unemployed university graduates;

■ Past integration policies have however not allowed Tunisia to diversify its partners and have produced negative side-effects and policy dilemmas examined in detail in chapter 2.

Tunisia's Global Integration Policies

Since the early 1970s, Tunisia's trade policy has rested on three pillars. The first is promoting exports, through generous incentives to attract foreign direct investments (FDI) in the "offshore" sector, incentives to exporting firms, and trade agreements. The second is protecting domestic industries and strictly regulating markets. However, a decisive move toward a market economy started in 1986, and a large number of structural reforms were introduced gradually: liberalizing tariffs and prices, privatizing state enterprises, reducing entry barriers to economic sectors and pre-authorizations, and enacting a new competition law. The third pillar is more recent, and concerns trade facilitation.

Export Promotion

Tunisia's first FDI and export promotion tools were put in place in 1972, with the establishment of an offshore regime, which provided generous fiscal and financial incentives to exporters (see below). In 1992, the fiscal and financial incentives to exporting firms (the offshore regime) were reinforced and streamlined into a comprehensive investment incentives code to boost FDI and exports and create jobs (Investment Incentive Code). The generous incentive system was deemed necessary to boost exports and foreign exchange earnings because the heavy protection of Tunisia's domestic market had created an anti-export bias. This heterodox trade policy stance is not unique to Tunisia, as many other countries, including Japan, Korea, Malaysia, and Mauritius, have used similar policy regimes. In the case of Tunisia, here are some examples of the numerous incentives provided to exporting firms:

■ Firms exporting at least 70 percent of their production are offered a 10-year corporate tax holiday after which they would face 50 percent of the standard corporate tax (35 percent);[10]

■ Exporting firms are exempted from customs tariffs for raw materials and equipments necessary for the export activity. Similarly, they enjoy duty exemption on capital goods that have no locally-made counterparts while the value-added tax (VAT) is limited to 10 percent on capital goods imports (1999 Budget Law provisions);

■ Foreign investors are free to transfer or repatriate their profits and enjoy tax relief on reinvested profits and income up to 35 percent of the income or profits subject to tax;

■ Foreign staff and investors or their foreign representatives in charge of managing a Tunisia-based company benefit from the payment of a 20 percent flat tax rate on gross income and enjoy an exemption of customs duties and comparable taxes.

---

10. As part of a December 2006 fiscal Law, exporting firms will face, starting in 2008, a flat 10 percent corporate tax while the standard corporate tax will be reduced to 30 percent.

Because the "offshore" regime is geographically neutral (no geographical restrictions), the government approved in 1992 a law for geographically bounded zones to boost regional industrial development, centered on regional comparative advantages. A few Special Economic Zones were then created, most notably in Bizerte in the north and in Zarzis in the south. The objective of the government was to help trigger FDI flows to these high-potential zones by offering economic incentives.[11] The latter include an exemption of taxes on profits or incomes, a suspension of the VAT on local purchases, an exemption of reinvested profits, duty-free imports of necessary raw materials and equipments, flexible labor contracts ("limited duration contract"), and a One-Stop-Shop to facilitate the administrative processes and recruitment process, assistance with staff recruitment, technical support and incorporation procedures of the activity on the market.

Further, to help exporters (especially the emerging ones) overcome information and other market failures inherent in penetrating new markets, various trade-support institutions, programs, and financing schemes were created. The programs are essentially geared toward supporting market search, market testing and market penetration through technical assistance, subsidies, matching grant schemes, information sharing and diffusion, etc. The Fonds de Promotion des Exportations (FOPRODEX or Export Promotion Fund), set up in 1985, grants loans and transport subsidies to exporters, carries out international market surveys, assists enterprises with canvassing and advertising, and helps them strengthen their internal structure. The Centre de Promotion des Exportation (CEPEX) provides a one-stop shop for exporters, implements the export promotion strategy under the Ministry of Trade, manages the computerized trade database Trade Net, and organizes training missions, in-country fairs, and exhibitions.[12]

As part of World Bank Tunisia's export development projects (I and II), two important programs aimed at tackling the difficulties new exporters face in identifying the right target market, the right product segment, the right selling channel and the extent of competition in that market as well as in accessing to working capital from banks were set up. The first, the Export Market Access Fund or FAMEX, is an innovative matching grant scheme that targets emerging exporters with export potential, firms exporting new products, and exporters seeking to penetrate new markets. It provides, on a demand-driven basis, a 50 percent non-reimbursable co-financing to help individual firms implement investments in market research and pre-competitive programs (establishment of export service offices abroad, search for partnerships, export plan-related training, product design modifications, etc.). FAMEX also provides 70 percent of co-financing to professional associations such as export associations, chambers of commerce, and professional consulting organizations, to support groups of Tunisian firms working under a specific common export plan and to support the institutional strengthening for export development of such entities.

---

11. The difference between the offshore and the Special Economic Zones in Tunisia (for example, Bizerte) is that the offshore is a regime applied to companies with no geographical restrictions, whereas a Special Economic Zone is a geographical limited area, a zone under a set of special rules.

12. Tunisia Trade Net is a data processing network that connects firms, freight forwarders and commissioners, customs agents, carriers and shipping agents to process electronically the various formalities of import and export. See below.

Following a successful first phase in 2000–05 (high demand from the private sector, US$ 418 million incremental exports and US$ 39 million tax receipts for an investment of US$ 11 million), Tunisia is implementing FAMEX II since 2006. The program has already surpassed its performance target of supporting 500 individual firms (100 of the US$ 17.6 million allocated to FAMEX II) and an additional financing of US$ 6 million is approved by the World Bank to assist 200 additional firms and maintain the momentum.

The second program, the Pre-shipment Export Finance Guarantees (PEFG), seeks to encourage financial institutions to provide pre-shipment working capital financing to emerging exporters with viable export contracts. Indeed, small and medium enterprises (SME) face a market failure resulting from asymmetry of information between Banks and exporters' regarding ability of the latter to execute export orders according to buyers' standards of quality, cost, and delivery (Alavi 2007). Tunisia's PEFG is designed to help alleviate this market failure by bearing a part of the nonperformance risk while the banks learn to know the abilities of the exporters and the seriousness of the buyers. As box 1.1 shows, its performance has however been mixed.

Finally, beyond the export promotion tools, the government has sometimes used heterodox export promotion policies at the sectoral level. A case in point is the deal struck with European automobile companies in 1995. The government decided to halt the assembly of private cars and negotiated with European automakers "local content rules" for the import of European cars. Starting 1998, foreign makers were authorized to export their vehicles to Tunisia only in exchange for purchasing motor vehicle components manufactured by the Tunisian firms. The government encouraged at the same time FDI in the car component sectors, by advertising the generous incentives granted by the offshore regime. And it worked. French, Italian and German carmakers responded by investing in Tunisia's car component sector and by partnering with Tunisia-based firms. The initial boom in Tunisia's export of parts and components to Europe was largely driven by this partnership (see below).

External Trade Liberalization

Although the level of protection of the Tunisian economy remains high (see the next section), policies over the last 10 years aimed at liberalizing trade. Tunisia's approach to liberalization has been "preferential" and "gradual." The country has signed a large number of Preferential Trade Agreement (PTA) and the focus has been on gradually dismantling tariffs faced by preferential partners under the context of these agreements. Most-Favored Nation (MFN) liberalization has been minimal, ad hoc and largely autonomous (outside of the WTO framework).

The hallmark of Tunisia's external liberalization strategy is the Association Agreement with the European Union. The latter is Tunisia's main economic partner, accounting for about 70 percent of Tunisia's imports and 80 percent of exports. One of the key objectives of the AA is to create a free trade area for industrial goods between Tunisia and the EU by 2008. Because Tunisia enjoys duty-free access to the EU since 1998, the onus was on the government to gradually cut tariffs on EU imports to zero by 2008. The agreed schedule has been rigorously followed, and tariffs on EU imports went from about 100 percent in 1996 to 4 percent in 2007. The Government is currently working on the last series of tariff

Box 1.1. The Mixed Performance of the PEFG in Tunisia

Tunisia's PEFG guarantees up to 90 percent—with an average of 50 percent—of the non-performance risks associated with pre-shipment export loans with maturities of up to 180 days, which were made by participating banks to ESEs. A premium of 0.15 percent per month was paid by the borrowers and was set at this level to ensure that it did not constitute a major financial burden on exporter. The scheme, which was administered by the Export Insurance Agency (COTUNACE), did not cover buyer nonpayment, buyer country risk, maritime disasters, and other risks.

The PEGF facility went through two distinct phases:

♦ *Stellar performance during the first six months.* During the first six months, the facility issued 43 guarantee certificates, exceeding performance targets for the facility for that time period (this represented $2 million of loans guaranteed and $3.4 million of additional exports generated). During that time, the management team was strong and proactively led by the chief executive officer (CEO) of COTUNACE. The team regularly visited enterprises and initiated the development of a risk information database on clients. As the head of the Risk Agreement Committee (RAC) of the Ministry of Finance, the CEO of COTUNACE ensured adherence to all of the operational modalities and principles for PEFGs. He also led an extensive marketing campaign and awareness building for banks and enterprises about the availability, objectives, and principles of PEFGs.

♦ *Sharp decline in performance following initial success.* Subsequently, the facility performed far below expectations. Six months into its operation, the facility's management team was replaced with a less-skilled team consisting of a part time manager with little institutional backing, no business plan, and no clear understanding of and commitment to the PEFG principles. The coverage and outreach of the facility declined and banks lost confidence that the facility to share nonperformance risks. Many banks reverted back to ex ante evaluation of nonperformance risks, which not only delayed the financing process, but also increased administrative costs and substantially reduced outreach to emerging exporters. The lack of proper supervision and follow-up by the PEFG management team even led a few banks to use PEFG as a supplemental guaranty for experienced exporters (one firm used it 28 times, and two others used it 18 times), instead of using it as a catalyst to help new exporters access pre-shipment finance. A decision by the RAC not to reimburse the banks for two cases of loan defaults due to the bad faith of the borrower also had a negative effect on the credibility of the PEFG scheme. At PEFG closing, out of a total of 57 claims, 27 were rejected, only 19 were fully repaid and 8 were still open.

The Tunisian experience shows that strong and credible management team cultivating good relations with financial institutions is critical for schemes similar to PEFGs that aim to serve as a catalyst to address export financing constraints. Proper promotion and marketing of the scheme is also important, particularly by the banks themselves, which are the ultimate beneficiaries of PEFGs. Another lesson learnt from the Tunisian experience is that the PEFG facilities must incorporate mechanisms to reduce the risk of loan misuse, but if there is a loan default due to bad faith of the borrower, the lending bank should be reimbursed by the facility. Finally, the PEFG coverage decisions should be based mainly on the underlying export transaction. Ex ante evaluation of exporters' manufacturing nonperformance risks would delay the process and counter the objectives of PEFGs.

Source: Alavi (2007).

reductions since in January 2008, when trade in industrial goods between Tunisia and the EU should be completely free of tariff.[13]

The steady reduction of tariffs on EU imports contrasts with slow reduction of the MFN tariffs (the ones faced by non-preferential partners), which stands at 24.7 percent in 2007. The large gap between Preferential and MNF tariffs creates a serious challenge for the government. Maintaining this gap may lead to trade diversion while providing an incentive for fraud (especially on the origin of products). At the same time, in contrast with the EU, Asian countries (that face the MFN tariffs) have generally lower prices and competitive exchange rates and may pose a more serious threat to Tunisian industries. The government has opted to pursue the dismantling of the MFN tariffs, but this is likely to be done in a gradual fashion.[14]

One of the key features of Tunisia's tariff dismantling approach is its strong linkage with an industrial upgrading program to prepare Tunisian firms for a more liberal and competitive environment. The industrial upgrading ("*mise a niveau*") program was put in place in 1996 as part of the liberalization process to enhance the organizational, technological, and marketing capabilities of firms being gradually exposed to competition vis-à-vis the EU. The goal was to strengthen their competitiveness by helping them invest in new equipment, training, organization, certification, license acquisition, financial restructuring, marketing and product quality enhancement. Indeed, about 90 percent of Tunisian firms are small and medium enterprises most of which are family-owned.

Today, more than 3500 manufacturing firms have participated in the MAN program. According to a recent evaluation, 76 percent of participating firms indicated that the MAN has allowed them to improve production processes (via investment in new equipments) and 52 percent of them responded that the MAN has helped them conquer new markets. However, most firms deplored the heavy bureaucracy associated with the program, and the fact that largest firms are the main beneficiaries. The lack of emphasis on immaterial investment and the limited financial support by the banks are also decried. That being said, 62 percent of participating firms declared being satisfied with the MAN (IEQ 2006a).[15]

To address some of the weaknesses of the MAN, the government launched in 2004 a more ambitious program called the *Programme de Modernisation Industrielle* (industrial

---

13. Duty-free access is however subject to compliance with rules of origin. In other words, the traded goods should be accepted as being originated from the partner country according to the ROO specified in the agreement. A product is said to originate in the free trade area or the preferential partner when it is grown, harvested, wholly produced, or "substantially transformed" in the free trade area or the partner. Under the AA, detailed ROO of origin are used (see section II). To benefit from cheaper inputs from the Euro-Med area while complying with the rules of origin of the AA with the EU, Tunisia has signed the Pan-Euro-Med protocol on ROO, which extends the scope for diagonal cumulation of origin to include the EU-25, EFTA countries, five western Balkan nations, and Turkey and Euro-Med AA countries. In other words, once ROO within the area are fully harmonized, a Tunisian exporter can purchase inputs from these countries, and still be eligible for duty-free entry on the final goods produced from those inputs.

14. Another challenge for the government is the liberalization of agriculture as part of the AA. Agriculture was indeed shielded from reciprocal liberalization and considered as "sensitive" by both the EU and Tunisia. The little in the way of liberalization in this sector consisted of enlarging gradually and bilaterally the quotas on trade of a specified list of products under specific periods, which provides only marginal opportunities for market access.

15. A more thorough analysis of the MAN is warranted. Techniques such as propensity score matching can be used to have a better handle of the potential selection bias inherent in the methodologies used by existing evaluations by the IEQ and by the *Agence Française de Development (AFD 2006)*.

modernization program or PMI).[16] This program, designed in cooperation with the EU, aims at providing technical assistance to support firm creation, innovation and quality enhancement. Parts of the program are geared toward improving the "environment" of firms, including strengthening certification and standard compliance processes and intellectual property right structures and mechanisms and participating to a credit warranty structure created in 2003 to enhance access to credit (SOTUGAR).[17] The whole program is managed by a small management committee in the Ministry of Industry comprising six Tunisian and six European experts supervised by 14 representatives of stakeholder organizations.

Finally beside the EU, Tunisia external trade liberalization has been pursued through PTAs with other regional entities and countries. Tunisia has signed a PTA with the Greater Arab Free Trade Area or GAFTA (18 Arab countries), two pluri-lateral agreements (the AGADIR agreement with Jordan, Morocco and Egypt and the agreement with the EFTA composed of Switzerland, Norway, Island and Liechtenstein), and six bilateral agreements with Morocco, Egypt, Jordan, Syria, Libya, Turkey.[18] The FTA with Turkey allows Tunisian firms to purchase cheap inputs from Turkey while still qualifying for duty-free entry in Europe.[19] As seen in the next section, contrary to the AA with the EU, the implementation of these agreements is quite complex and largely ineffective.

Trade Facilitation

The efficient global integration needed for strong export performance depends not only on the trade regime, but also on formalities in port logistics, customs clearance, and quality and safety controls, all of which affect transaction costs. Improving the trade regime without addressing basic trade facilitation issues may maintain excessive costs and time to trade and diminish the potential effects of trade liberalization on output, job and income. For Tunisian exporters in the largest exporting industries (T&C and MEE), fast, efficient and just-in-time access to European markets is perhaps the most crucial factor of competitiveness. Excessive trade logistics costs and inefficiencies are a recipe for losing market shares for these and many other industries. Yet, the costs of trade transactions represent a heavier burden on emerging SME onshore firms.

Trade facilitation has received much emphasis since 2000, when the government adopted a comprehensive approach to the issue. Beyond trade-related documentation processing, the country sought to improve trade facilitation through streamlined technical controls, improved customs procedures, and increased access to information on standards and technical regulations to raise transparency and meet international trade obligations.

---

16. This program was financed in part by €50 million from MEDA, EU's principal financial instrument for the implementation of the Euro-Mediterranean Partnership.

17. The PMI will also participate with €9 million as a shareholder in the *Société Tunisienne de Garantie*. This was created in 2003 to provide various forms of credit guarantee for the small and medium sized industry sector.

18. Tunisia has signed a preferential agreement with the European Free Trade Area (Suisse, Norvège, Islande, Liechtenstein) in 2004. This agreement entered into force in 1998. It proposes to replicate the Tunisia-EU AA reciprocal commitments to AFTA countries.

19. Turkey is in a customs union with the EU and can export "made-in-Europe" inputs (such as fabrics) at lower prices than the EU-15.

The World Bank Export Development Project I and II supported much of the measures taken. Because the procedures for external trade in Tunisia require the processing of documents by multiple agencies—the Ministry of Commerce, banks, the port authority, and customs, as well as the usual professional organizations such as customs brokers, shipping agents, and freight forwarders, use of IT was considered as crucial to automate workflows and clearance procedures.

Today, Tunisia has succeeded in applying IT to the whole range of trade documents and procedures, which helps simplify procedures and automate trade documentation and customs requirements. Just as it did in countries like Singapore and Mauritius, e-government has allowed a reduction in time to trade and reduced transactions costs for exporters. In the late 1990s, there were 19 distinct steps involved in an import transaction and 15 steps in an export transaction, translating into an average of 8 days required for trade document processing (and in some cases up to 18 days). Today, the number of procedures involved in imports and exports have been cut to 7 and 5, respectively (Doing Business 2008). Trade document processing can now be done in 2 days. The Trade Net's electronic data interchange capabilities have helped improve the efficiency and speed of trade procedures in Tunisia.

Progress has also been made in reducing the complexity and cost of technical controls over the last 2 years. Before 2005, procedures for imports were lengthy and complex and constituted one of the main factors responsible for delaying the clearance of goods. As part of the EDP II, technical controls were simplified and automated and as a result, technical standards for imported goods are now reduced to about 5 percent of goods of mass consumption. In addition, a technical barrier to trade (TBT) enquiry point is established in the Standards and Intellectual Property Institute (INORPI) in an effort to promote transparency in technical regulations.

However, despite the significant reduction in document processing time in the last two years, there remain inefficiencies in the country's international supply chain and Tunisian exporters are still missing export opportunities. The country has only a few large modern warehouses and logistics services, provided by small-atomized entities, do not match the need of the private sectors. And logistics costs are high. They reach 17 percent of the sale value in the chemical and pharmaceutical industries, and 13 percent in the distribution sector (World Bank 2007). The incidence of logistics costs for firms in some segments of the automotive parts industry operating on a just-in-time basis is estimated to be way above international standard, penalizing Tunisian exporters (World Bank 2005). The Tunisian market is characterized by scattered wholesale distributors and small warehouses, which result in costly and inefficient wholesale trade and has a direct impact on export competitiveness, as it increases costs and delays for producers.

A Remarkable Performance of Manufacturing Sectors

A Rapid Response of FDI

The fiscal and financial incentives of the offshore sector have let to an important increase in FDI. Annual FDI flows increased steadily from less than TD 100 million in the 1980s to TD 316 million in 1990–95, TD 558 million in 1996–2000 and TD 845 million in 2001–05. In the latter period, FDI represented 2.8 percent of GDP, against 2.1 percent in 1990–95 (Figure 1.1).

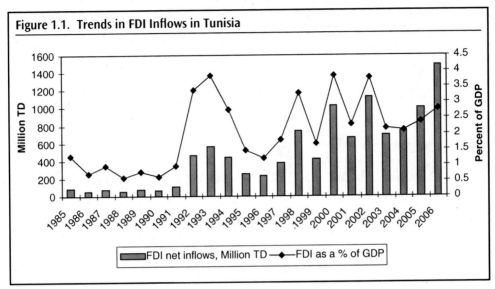

Figure 1.1. Trends in FDI Inflows in Tunisia

Source: Foreign Investment Promotion Agency, Tunisia.

Clearly, privatization of state-owned enterprises (cement factories, hotels, banks, and telecom) has played a role in some of the recent surges in FDI. Still, today, most of the largest and most dynamic enterprises in the manufacturing sector are organized under the "wholly exporting" regime indicating that the offshore regime has clearly been the most important driver of "green field" FDI in the economy. In 1992, 81 percent of FDI flows went to the energy sector and only 3 percent to the manufacturing sector. Following the enacting of the investment incentives code in 1992, FDI flows to the manufacturing sector increased dramatically. Between 1992 and 2001, 30 percent of FDI went to the manufacturing sector against 51 percent in energy and 7 percent in services. FDI flows to services started increasing in 2002 mostly thanks to market opening in telecom (second mobile license to ORASCOM) and privatization in banking. Today, services accounts for 25 percent of FDI inflows in Tunisia.[20]

Within manufacturing, FDI in the textiles and clothing and electrical and mechanical engineering increased dramatically but in a sequential manner. In the early 1990s, 60 percent of FDI flows to the manufacturing sector went to T&C and only 12 percent to the mechanical and electrical engineering sectors (Figure 1.2). But trends reversed in recent years and the machinery and electrics sector has now overtaken T&C as the largest recipient of FDI. In 2001–06, this sector claimed 31 percent of total FDI in manufacturing, against 24 percent for T&C. The main feature of the FDIs in the above sectors is that they reflect mostly new ("green field") productive capital injected in the economy. In contrast, a large part of the recent FDI flows to the construction materials sector reflect the privatization of public cement companies. Privatization started in the late 1990s and today only 2 out of the seven formal firms are public.

---

20. Excluding the partial (35 percent of capital) privatization of the state telecommunications company *Tunisie Telecom,* which brought US$2.35 billion (7.5 percent of GDP) to the state's coffers. This amounts to more than the cumulated revenues of all privatization operations since 1987.

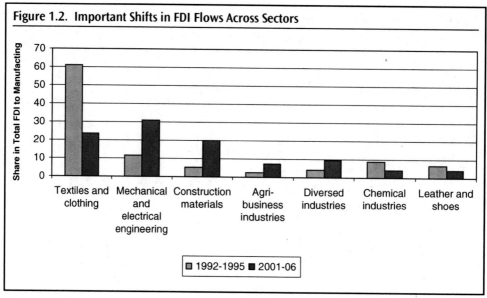

Figure 1.2. Important Shifts in FDI Flows Across Sectors

Source: Foreign Investment Promotion Agency, Tunisia.

A Rapid Rise in Manufacturing Exports and a Diversification Away from Fuel

As a result of increased investments, first in T&C and later in mechanical and electrical engineering, exports of manufacturing products increased dramatically. In particular, the integration policies led to a rapid development of the T&C sector, as a large number of European textile companies sub-contract the assembly segment of their business to Tunisia, triggering a tremendous growth in exports of textile products and a diversification of exports (Figures 1.3 and 1.4). The share of textiles and clothing in exports rose from 18 percent of total merchandise exports in 1980 to 33 percent in 2006, while that of fuel plummeted from 52 percent to 13 percent (Figure 1.4). This rapid diversification away from energy toward labor-intensive manufactures has been associated with higher productivity (Nabli and others 1999).

T&C is now a mature industry in Tunisia and investments flowing to the sector have diminished significantly since the beginning of the years 2000 as seen above. Furthermore, Tunisia's preferences in the European market have eroded with the removal of the Multi-Fiber Arrangement (MFA) under the Agreement on Textile and Clothing (ATC) on January 1, 2005. The lifting of all T&C quotas has resulted in a significant price decline of T&C products, benefiting consumers worldwide, and has brought tremendous pressures on retailers, distributors and producers alike. Some of the most efficient and formerly quota-restricted countries, such as China and India, have gained increased market shares in major importing markets.

Still, Tunisia has resisted so far very well against competition from China as Tunisia has managed to maintain its market share in Europe in spite of stiffer competition (World Bank 2006a).[21] A World Bank (2006a) report shows that the EU market requires fast turn-

---

21. It should be noted however that both the US and the EU have reinstated quotas against China in 2005 following a dramatic surge of Chinese exports to these markets. However, these quotas are to be removed in 2008 and the competition will be stiffer then.

around, and is less reliant on huge orders that are typical of U.S. retailers. These characteristics tend to favor efficient and specialized proximate suppliers such as Tunisia, with the ability to respond quickly to orders and to cut lead-time. The report showed that Tunisia is competitive in exporting time-sensitive, replenishable products in the EU market because its ability to reach European markets in two days (against three weeks for maritime shipment from Asia) means lower inventory costs and risks for retailers in Europe. Proximate countries such as Morocco, Turkey, Romania, and Bulgaria were identified as the most serious direct competitors of Tunisia in Europe (World Bank 2006a).

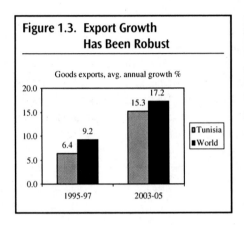

Figure 1.3. Export Growth Has Been Robust

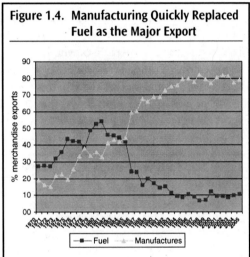

Figure 1.4. Manufacturing Quickly Replaced Fuel as the Major Export

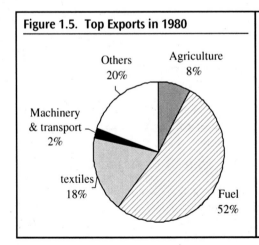

Figure 1.5. Top Exports in 1980

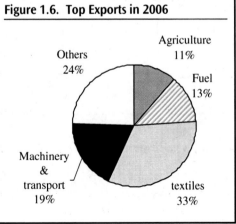

Figure 1.6. Top Exports in 2006

An Impressive Growth of Mechanical and Electrical Engineering Industries

Since 1997, a second wave of structural transformation is occurring in the industry. This followed the government's decision to halt the assembly of private cars and negotiate with European automakers "local content rules" for the import of European cars. This decision led to the initial growth of the mechanical and electrical engineering (MEE) sector and strengthened vertical integration with the EU car industry.

The broad category "MEE" includes a large number of products produced by the auto- mobile and electrical industries: electrical wiring systems, electrical motors and generators, wheels and rubber tires, plastic auto components as well as various mechanical auto parts. Since the late 1990s, exports of MEE products are witnessing annual growth rates in the 12–17 percent range. This dramatic growth propelled this sector as the second largest driver of manufacturing performance in Tunisia (after T&C). Indeed, the share of "machinery and electrics" in total exports has increased from 9.5 percent in 1995 to around 19 percent in 2005.

The electrical wiring system is by far the largest and most dynamic sub-sector of the MEE industry. It represents 74 percent of sectoral output and 73 percent of the exports of Tunisia's MEE sector. About 62 percent of wholly exporting firms of the MEE operate in the electrical wiring sector.[22] Tunisia is now of Europe's top 10 suppliers of electrical wiring systems and the country's global market share in this segment is about 2.2 percent. Thanks to the rapid growth of exports in recent years, the share of parts and component in Tunisia's total export has surpassed the average for the world's 16 highest trade performers (Figure 1.7).[23]

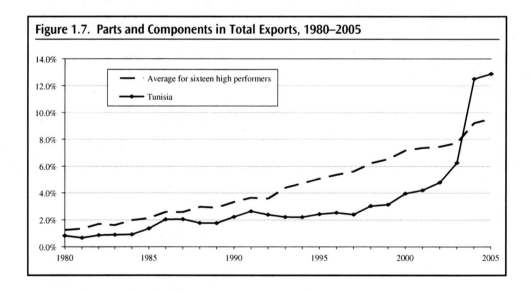

Figure 1.7. Parts and Components in Total Exports, 1980–2005

A Good Resistance of Most Other Industries in Spite of Increasing Difficulties

While manufacturing exports and employment are largely driven by the T&C and MEE sectors in Tunisia, construction materials, chemicals, agro-processing and other indus- tries play an important role in sustaining value-addition and employment in Tunisia (see

---

22. This is in contrast with only two wholly exporting firms operating in the home electrical appli- ances sub-sector.

23. The 16 high performers are the group of non-oil exporters, non-transition countries that achieved more than 4.5 per cent of average annual GDP growth since 1980—Botswana, Burkina Faso, Cambodia, Chile, China, India, Indonesia, Republic of Korea, Malaysia, Mauritius, Pakistan, Singapore, Sri Lanka, Taiwan, Thailand, and Uganda.

figures 1.8 and 1.9). Whether the above industries, in particular those established on the basis of an "import-substitution" model would be able to withstand stiffer competition was a major cause of concern 10 years ago. Indeed, some industries, such as non-phosphate chemicals, household appliance and consumer electronics sectors were particularly vulnerable to tariff dismantling. Ten years later, the numbers point to a good resistance of most of these sectors.

The *construction materials* sector—one of the country's highest value-added sectors—witnessed an annual growth rate of 4.1 percent over the 2002–2006 period.[24] The cement and limes sub-sector has performed particularly well thanks to the booming construction sector, and is likely to grow even faster in the future in connection with the large infrastructure projects planned in the 11th plan. In 2006, cement and limes realized 32 percent of the building material sector exports. Thanks to the privatization of formerly state-owned firms, private firms now dominate the sub-sector. Today only two out of the seven formal firms are public.[25] The ceramic and tiles sub-sector, the other important segment of building material face stiffer competition but is resisting so far quite well. In 2006, the sector realized 29 percent of the building material sector's exports.[26]

The *chemical* sector (2–3 percent of GDP) has also resisted stagnation overall (2.4 percent annual growth over 2002–2006), thanks in part to high international prices of phosphates and phosphate-based fertilizers, which dominate the sector. Tunisia remains the world's fifth largest phosphate exporter and is among the countries having the largest percentage of raw phosphate transformed into fertilizers (85 percent). A number of firms have emerged as dynamic players seeking regional expansion in the chemical components for detergents (polyphosphates). Furthermore, the dynamism of mechanical and electrical engineering is driving growth in the plastics sub-sector, where many firms (65) are exporters to Libya, France and Italy.[27] Still, it is not clear whether the sector can resist dismantling of tariffs vis-à-vis non preferential partners such as China.

Similarly, while the overall annual growth of *agri-business* stands at 3.9 percent since 2002, the sector faces major challenges and weaknesses in spite of a delayed opening. In export markets (olive oil, fish and seafood and dates), Tunisia's market shares are below potential because of constraints such as market positioning, marketing, and quality assurance[28] (see World Bank 2006b). For the import-substitute segments of the sector (dairy, beverages, confectionary, etc.), while competition from Europe is increasing in many areas (for example, confectionary, non-milk dairy such as yoghourt, cheese and ice cream), overall competitive pressure is limited by the heavy concentration of the sector (dominance of large family-owned conglomerates) and the complexities of tariff dismantling in agro-processing. Indeed, the government has delayed the tariff reduction on agro-business final products because agro-business firms would be strangled by high-priced inputs (because of agricultural protection) and low-priced output in the absence of liberalization of agriculture. In other

---

24. This sector benefits from large deposits of primary inputs (sand, clay, silicates, gypsum, etc.) in the country.

25. Prices of cement are however not fully liberalized.

26. Fifty percent of exports are shipped to Libya and 16 percent to France.

27. Most of the exporting firms are affiliates of foreign firms also present in the electrical and automotive industry.

28. Olive oil employs 250,000 people, represents 30 percent of arable land and accounts for 0.5–6 percent of manufacturing exports depending on the years.

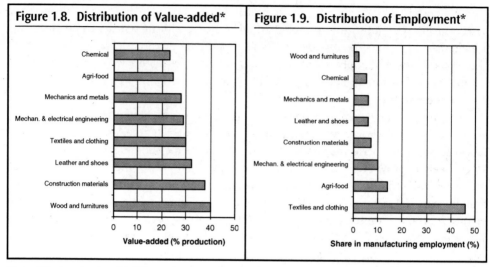

Figure 1.8. Distribution of Value-added*

Value-added (% production)

Figure 1.9. Distribution of Employment*

Share in manufacturing employment (%)

Note: *Sectors having 10,000 employees or less (such as plastics and paper packaging) are left out.
Source: Institut National Statistique, Tunisia.

words, because agriculture is by and large shielded from liberalization within the Tunisia-EU AA, agribusiness firms would be unable to compete if only the industrial component of tariffs were liberalized within this framework.

How did most Tunisian industries manage to maintain competitiveness? At least four factors have played a role:

- The tariff dismantling of the "sensitive" sectors is quite recent and is incomplete in many sectors. Indeed, tariff dismantling begun with capital goods and input (1996) and primary raw materials and intermediate products (1996–2000) so that its initial effect was to increase the effective protection of firms. Elimination of tariff on goods produced locally was scheduled to take place during 2000–2007 in the AA tariff dismantling scheme and is still ongoing in a few most "sensitive" industries.[29]
- EU final manufacturing products, which enjoy better access to the Tunisian markets since 2000, generally bears a quality premium and are more expensive than locally manufactured goods. In other words, product differentiation has allowed more affluent consumers in Tunisia to access better quality products while permitting domestic firms to continue securing a segment of the domestic market.
- The Tunisian dinar depreciated steadily vis-à-vis the Euro since 2001. As a result, Tunisia's nominal and real effective exchange rates declined by 8 and 7 percent respectively between 2001 and 2007, thereby helping maintain competitiveness.
- Finally, Tunisian firms have reacted to the liberalization by adopting various strategies supported by programs such as the MAN, the PMI and trade-support programs. Outside the highly specialized sector of MEE, a large portion of Tunisian firms in other industries have attempted to diversify their products, enhance quality to

---

29. Locally manufactured goods considered as capable of facing up stiffer competition were liberalized in the 1996–2007 period.

differentiate products, and sought to diversify their markets. In the IEQ's 2006 enterprise survey, 44 percent of firms declared having deployed efforts to diversify and differentiate products. Efforts aimed at diversifying markets were less prevalent, with 37 percent of firms involved in such a strategy. Tunisian firms also invested in R&D (40 percent of firms), quality control (71 of firms declare having a quality control unit), information technology (79 percent of firms connected to the Internet on average) and vocational training (68 percent of firms).

A Positive Impact on Employment

The ultimate goal of Tunisia's integration policies is to create jobs. One way to determine whether integration policies have effectively created jobs is to focus on the offshore "sector," where generous incentives were provided to investors and exporters. Clearly, available figures point to a dramatic increase in employment in the offshore sector, especially since 1992 when the investment incentive code was enacted. In 1980, 8 years after the creation total employment in the offshore sector was about 10,000; in 1990, it employed 70,000 workers and; today, with more than 245,000 persons working under that regime, the offshore "sector" represents 54 percent of total manufacturing jobs and 8 percent of all jobs in the country.

Table 1.1 shows the distribution of employment in the offshore sector in 2006. Almost 90 percent of all the jobs in the offshore "sector" are in manufacturing. With the exception of tourism, the service sector has a very small number of firms operating under the offshore regime and thus represents a tiny fraction of total employment in that regime. Within manufacturing, as in the case of FDI and exports, T&C and MEE claim the bulk of job creations. T&C and MEE account for close to 60 percent and 14 percent of offshore manufacturing jobs respectively. Because more than 80 percent of workers in T&C are women, Tunisia's integration policies have been favorable to women. In other words, they have helped employ low-skilled women who otherwise would have been unemployed or would earn lower incomes in agriculture or the urban informal sector. On the other hand, sectors such as construction materials and chemicals account for a much smaller fraction of offshore jobs, showing the inward orientation of these sectors.

Table 1.1. Employment in the Offshore Sector in 2006

Sector	Number of Jobs	%	Manufacturing Branch	Number of Jobs	%
Manufacturing	216489	89	Textiles and clothing	126648	58.5
Non-tourism services	7402	1.9	Electronics & electrics	30656	14.2
Tourism	16951	6.9	Leather, footwear	17221	7.9
Agriculture	1733	0.7	Other Industries	17610	8.1
Energy	3250	1.3	Metallurgy and mechanics	9672	4.4
			Chemical	7753	3.5
			Construction materials	6929	3.2
Total	245825	100	Total	216489	100

Source: Ministry of Employment, Tunisia.

Is the offshore sector creating high-skilled jobs? The question is pointed because Tunisia's unemployment rate is particularly high among educated individuals between ages 25 and 29 (20 percent) and individuals below age 25 (30 percent). Indeed, a recent tracer study shows that over 45 percent of higher education graduates from the 2004 cohort were unemployed 18 after receiving their diploma. Moreover, many take jobs that do not use or underutilize their skills. Whether the offshore sector creates jobs for high-skilled job seekers also deserves an investigation because more than half of offshore firms are in the clothing business, especially in down-market apparel assembly (subcontracting) where jobs are mostly for low-skilled workers. Indeed, this is a segment with low entry requirements in terms of technology, skills and capital, as well as sourcing and marketing expertise. The dominant segment of the MEE (electrical wiring) presents similar characteristics.

To examine the issue, one can decompose exports to see whether the products requiring special, specialized and sophisticated skills are becoming more or less prominent in Tunisia's exports (changes in the country's specialization). Here, the decomposition of exports is done according to their content classified by factor of competitiveness as proposed by the UNCTAD. The UNCTAD's categorization is useful in that it helps gauge specialization in relation with considerations relating to a country's underlying factor of competitiveness (UNCTAD 2002). Six products categories are distinguished:

- Differentiated products associated with specialized supplier networks such as non-electrical machinery; electrical machinery and communications equipment;
- "Science-based" manufactures (aircraft, computers and office equipment, pharmaceuticals and scientific instruments);[30]
- Scale-intensive manufacturing which includes paper, chemical excluding pharmaceutical, rubber and plastic products, iron and steel, road motor vehicles, ships and other transport equipment;
- Labor-intensive products such as leather, textiles, apparel, footwear, fabricated metal products and other manufactures;
- Resource-intensive manufacturing which comprises woods products and non-metallic mineral products; and
- Non-fuel primary commodities.

Figure 1.10 shows the decomposition of Tunisia's export according to the above grouping. Clearly, while low-skilled labor-intensive products still overwhelmingly dominate Tunisia's exports, the share of the latter in total exports have decreased quite significantly over the last 10 years. In 1995, 53 percent of total exports were constituted of low-skilled labor-intensive products. In 2005, this percentage has declined to 40 percent.

---

30. Exporting scale-intensive goods allows firms to reduce costs by extending plant size and lengthening production runs, while exporting science-based products allows them to spread the high fixed costs associated with research and development over a larger market. The science-based category recorded the strongest rate of export value growth over the last 25 years for both world exports and exports from developing countries, followed by the differentiated product category (i.e. products associated with specialized supplier networks). World exports of the science-based category grew about six-fold during this period compared to a 21-fold increase in the value of this category's exports from developing countries. Given that computers and office equipment (SITC 75) is included in the science-based category and that an important item of this product division refers to parts and components (SITC 759), it is likely that the very rapid export value growth of science-based exports from developing countries reflects the increased importance of international production sharing.

Yet, the expansion of the electrical, electronic and automobile components industry is beginning to slowly change the nature of labor demand toward higher skilled workers. The share of science-based exports and differentiated products in total exports has been slowly increasing since 1998 while that of labor-intensive products decreased. However, the share of the science-based category was almost insignificant in 1995, thus the rapid growth of the category is partly explained by the fact that it started from a low base. The most significant structural change that is occurring is thus the increase in the share of products whose manufacturing require specialized skills. Export of higher-skill and higher-technology products such as machineries, automobile parts and components are growing rapidly, from a very low base.[31]

A main challenge is to facilitate a rapid expansion of science-based, differentiated and scale-intensive products to accelerate technological development and employ university graduates that have the required skills.

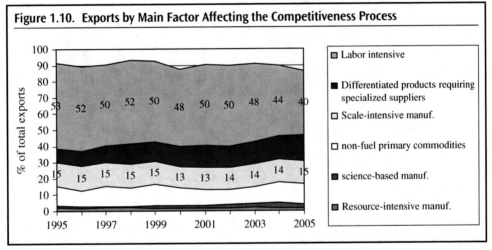

Figure 1.10. Exports by Main Factor Affecting the Competitiveness Process

Note: Categories based on UNCTAD (2002), Dynamic Productions in World Exports.
Source: Bank staff calculations based on UN Comtrade, UNTAD.

A Heavy Concentration on a Few Markets

Tunisia is heavily dependent on a few EU markets. About 71 percent of its export is shipped in four countries in Europe: France (33 percent), Italy (24 percent), Germany (8 percent) and Spain (5 percent). Over the past decade, exports to France and Italy, Tunisia's two largest export markets, have grown at a faster pace than the overall import growth in these countries, resulting in a 30 percent increase in market share in both markets (Figure 1.11). However, this performance has not allowed Tunisia to increase its world market share, which remained quasi-constant in this period.

Tunisia's integration with fast-growing East Asia is insignificant while integration with the United States declined sharply. Trade with MENA and SSA partners is growing but still

---

31. The inputs used in the production process are however almost entirely imported. The share of "machinery and electrics" in total imports accounted for 29 percent of Tunisia's total imports in 2005, up from 26 in 1995.

limited. Yet, in 2005, about 83 percent of the increase in global demand stemmed from non-EU, non-MENA markets (Figure 1.13). While the EU will remain critical for Tunisian exporters as well as a crucial source of global knowledge and technologies, there is scope for Tunisia to exploit the opportunities in large developing countries, whose formidable growth requires significant increases in imports (Figure 1.14). The large developing countries such as China and India that have become true global players in recent years offer a route to reduce dependence on slower growing EU markets. Beyond constituting important potential markets, countries like China and India can be important sources of FDI as Tunisia is an attractive export platform to the larger European market.[32]

Figure 1.11. Export Performance in the European Market

	share to total merchandise EXP	Tunisia's Market share	
	2005	1995	2005
World	**100**	**0.12**	**0.11**
4 EU total	**71**	**0.38**	**0.42**
of which			
France	33	0.59	0.74
Italy	24	0.60	0.75
Germany	8	0.20	0.13
Spain	5	0.21	0.22

Figure 1.12. Destination of Exports and Origin of Imports

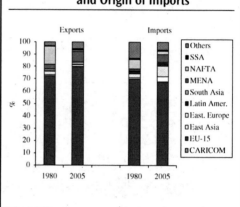

Source: COMTRADE.

Figure 1.13. Much of the Growth in the Global Demand Stems from Non-E.U. Markets

EU: 1995 = 23.9, 2005 = 17.3
Non EU: 1995 = 76.1, 2005 = 82.7
MENA: 1995 = 0.053, 2005 = 0.031

Figure 1.14. Opportunities Offered by Large Developing Country Markets are Huge

Share in world imports (%) for Brazil, China, India, US (1990 and 2005)

---

32. Such partnership seems to progress in the Pharmaceutical sector with India. A Tunisia-India Joint Working Group on Drugs and Pharmaceuticals has been created to explore opportunities for joint-ventures with major Indian Pharmaceutical firms such as Ranvaxy, Cipla and Hetero Drugs. The objective is to set up factories in Tunisia to supply the domestic market and to export duty-free to the EU.

In 2005, Tunisia has shipped only 8 percent of its exports to other MENA partners. On the import side, only 6.4 percent of its imports came from the region (Figures 1.12). With the MENA, while both Tunisia and Morocco are well-connected to EU production networks, there is very little cross-border trade in components for products subsequently exported to the EU. There is virtually no correlation between intra-regional export and exports to the EU. Yet, the location decisions of multinationals are crucially affected by the scope for effective sourcing of inputs and the ability to move inputs quickly and cheaply across national boundaries (World Bank 2006c). Participation to regional production network is at the heart of some recent regional drives such as in East Asia where they have contributed significantly to growth (Haddad 2007; World Bank 2007). The reform agenda in the area of trade policy, customs reforms and transport infrastructure is crucial in that respect (see below). Lack of progress on that front could undermine any cost advantages that a region may possess and reduce its attractiveness to multinational enterprises when it comes to investment and input sourcing decisions. Tunisia's rapid integration with Libya and, to a lesser degree, Morocco, is however promising both in terms of positioning Tunisia as an export platform and for increasing the scope for realizing economies of scale.

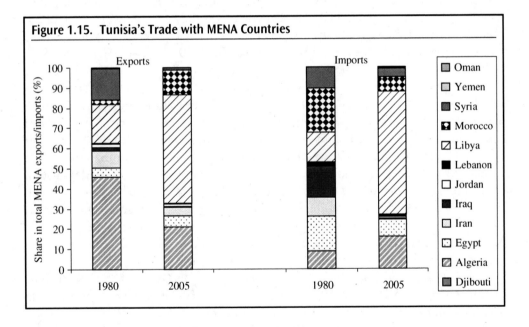

Figure 1.15. Tunisia's Trade with MENA Countries

Tunisia's trade with Africa is very limited, accounting for only 1.3 and 0.5 percent of Tunisia's exports and imports respectively. Yet, according to the World Bank's Global Economic Prospects 2007, GDP in Sub-Saharan Africa expanded by an estimated 5.3 percent in 2006. Oil-exporting economies are expected to grow 6.9 percent in 2007, about the same as last year. Among oil importers (excluding South Africa), the expansion has been sustained, and growth is estimated to have increased 4.7 percent. The regional expansion is broadly based, with a third of the countries experiencing growth in excess of 5 percent. Among oil exporters, growth was particularly strong in Angola (16.9 percent), Sudan (11.8 percent), and Mauritania (17.9 percent), which began oil production in February 2006. In addition to a strong expansion in oil production, buoyant domestic demand is projected to spur rapid growth in the non-oil sectors of most oil-exporting countries. GDP growth for the region as a whole is projected to remain broadly stable, coming in at about 5.4 percent in 2008. SSA is already a growing market for Tunisia's engineering, health and education services. Exploiting the trade potential in manufacturing, so far untapped, could yield important benefits for Tunisia (market, internationalization of Tunisian firms, and so forth).

Poor Performance in Integrating Non-Tourism Services

Services in Tunisia contribute nearly 60 percent of GDP, a level higher than the middle-income average of 53 percent but much lower than in the OECD countries (70 percent). If one excludes the services provided by the public administration, commercial services account for 47 percent of GDP in Tunisia. Of this, 25 percent is commerce, 16 percent is hotel & restaurants, 15 percent is transport, 13 percent is communication services, 8 percent is financial services and the rest a long list of disparate and not well-structured services.

More than 60 percent of the workforce (excluding agriculture) works in the services, and over the past five years, employment in services has grown at 17 percent a year, while manufacturing jobs have declined. Between years 2000 and 2005, the services sector has created 55,539 net jobs (75 percent of the total). Only in 2005 did the share of jobs created by the services sector fall due to an impressive expansion in the numbers of jobs in the agricultural sector—close to 79,000. Construction, transport and communications have been the most dynamic sectors in terms of job creation.

Following global trends, services have enjoyed a steady average annual growth rate of 5.9 percent over the last 10 years. Communications services (computers, IT services, and telecommunications and call centers) have more than tripled in size, from 1.3 percent of GDP to 4.3 percent. The robust growth is attributable in significant part to the growth in investment (including FDI) and capital accumulation in the sector. Gross capital formation in communications has tripled since 1990, reaching 7.4 percent of total gross investment. From 45 percent of the gross capital formation in 1990, the service sector now absorbs 53 percent of total gross investment in Tunisia. These investments in turn reflect the gradual liberalization of the sector, including the partial opening of the mobile segment and the partial privatization of Tunisia Telecom, the historical provider.

Yet, Tunisia is far from exploiting all the potential of the sector. The share of commercial services in GDP is low compared to the lower-tier of OEDC countries and emerging countries. Furthermore, 80 percent of Tunisia's services export revenues come from tourism, travel and transport services.[33] Tunisia has not yet taken advantage of the formidable growth in global services trade in recent years. Between 1995 and 2005 its exports of services grew by a mere 2.5 percent annually, about one-third that of the average middle-income country (figure 1.16). Almost all MENA countries did better than Tunisia. The region as a whole averaged an annual growth of 12 percent, with countries like Morocco, Lebanon, and Algeria enjoying above-average growth rates.

In light of the limited diversification of services exports, the overall poor performance of the services exports is mainly driven by tourism. As a result of sluggish growth in Tunisia and

---

33. Tourism accounts for 53 percent and transport 16 percent of services exports.

good performance in most medium-income countries, Tunisia's share in the world tourism exports declined from an average 0.20 percent in 1995–97 to 0.15 percent in 2003–05. The overall performance parallels this as shown by Figure 1.17 which compares Tunisia with the world's top 16 performers in services exports. From the same position as Tunisia in 1980, the market share of the world's top 16 performers in service exports grew rapidly, at a more or less steady rate over the last 25 years, in sharp contrast with Tunisia, whose market share declined (Figure 1.17).

The government's objective is to increase the share of commercial service in GDP from 47 to 57 percent over the next 10 years. To achieve this, it will be necessary to (i) open up further the backbone services to competition to increase investments, reduce the cost of services and further facilitate (and enable) exports of services and goods; The partial liberalization of the telecom sector in Tunisia illustrates the potential benefits of services opening. Thanks to reforms in this sector, massive investments have been undertaken to extend telecom networks and adopt new technologies, resulting in lower prices of telecom services and greater penetration of mobile services (15-folds increase over the last four years). As a result, Tunisia is now better-placed to compete in the business process outsourcing of a range of services (see Chapter 3). As seen below, further liberalization of the telecom sector will increase the possibilities of exporting new services. While reforms in telecom are well underway, many restrictions to entry and competition still remain in other sectors. The Institut d'Economie Quantitative (IEQ)'s 2006 annual report on competitiveness identifies the financial, telecom and air transport sectors as representing "major" constraints to a large number of firms in Tunisia. Chapter 3 looks identify some key reforms that could help harness the potential of services in Tunisia.

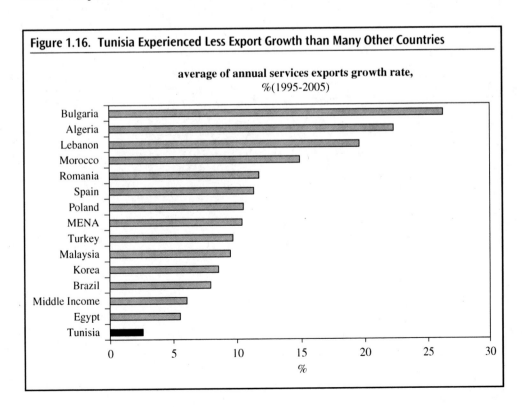

Figure 1.16. Tunisia Experienced Less Export Growth than Many Other Countries

average of annual services exports growth rate, %(1995-2005)

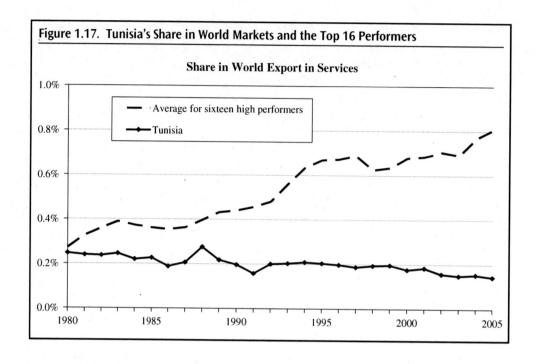

Figure 1.17. Tunisia's Share in World Markets and the Top 16 Performers

Share in World Export in Services

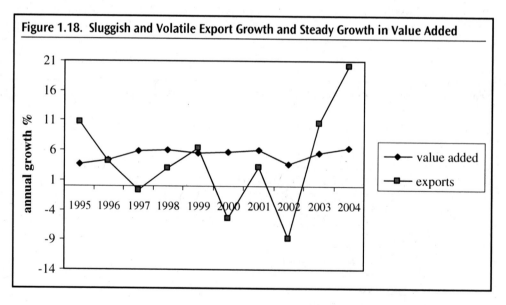

Figure 1.18. Sluggish and Volatile Export Growth and Steady Growth in Value Added

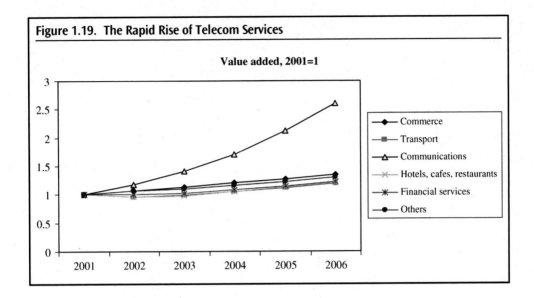

Figure 1.19. The Rapid Rise of Telecom Services

CHAPTER 2

Remaining Integration Challenges and Reform Options in the Goods Sector

W hile integration policies in Tunisia's industrial sector has led to impressive results, some key challenges lie ahead. These challenges relate to:

■ *The need to correct two distortions that have resulted from past integration policies: important tariff gaps and a dichotomy between the offshore and offshore sectors.* Indeed, Tunisia's trade opening approach has been preferential (its opens up vis-à-vis preferential partners and maintains a high protection vis-à-vis non-preferential partners) and the country now faces a dilemma: maintaining the current large gap between preferential and the (misnamed) "most-favored nation" tariffs may fuel fraud and a parallel market, while reducing the gap may hurt production and jobs. At the same time, with the increasing openness of the onshore sector to international competition, the former anti-export bias in trade policy is vanishing and the incentive gap between offshore and onshore sectors is turning discriminatory.

■ *The need to further improve the country's competitive position in the Euro-Med area to boost investments and diversify exports.* First, Tunisia's competitors in the region are catching up fast in terms of attracting foreign direct investments; second, while Tunisia has low factor costs (labor, energy, land, and so forth) and moderate transport costs, logistics services and constraints should be addressed to enhance connectivity with the global market and attract new investments; finally, further improvement in innovation and technological development is necessary.

This chapter derives some specific recommendations aimed at addressing the above challenges.

Tunisia's Current Integration Challenges

The Distortions Created by Past Integration Policies

Tunisia's past integration policies have well served the country as they allowed Tunisia to boost FDI, exports and job creation in the offshore sector as seen in chapter 1. However, after almost 10 years of trade liberalization in the industrial sector, the side effects of past policies are becoming stark. In particular, the preferential approach to liberalization (opening up vis-à-vis the EU while maintaining the MFN tariff at a high level) has created a gap in tariff, leading to greater incentive for fraud (and parallel market activities). At the same time, as the onshore sector has become more open to competition, the rationale for maintaining a large gap in the regulatory framework for investment and doing business between the offshore and the onshore sectors have greatly weakened.

Preferential liberalization has created important gaps between various tariffs. The Tunisian government has moved gradually toward simplifying the regime by reducing the number of rates and reducing tariff peaks in recent years. Since 2003, each annual Budget Law has included a reduction in the number of tariff rates. Thus, from 54 in 2003, the number of rate has been reduced to 17 in 2004, 14 in 2005, and 11 in 2006. The maximum tariffs rates of 100 and 150 percent were brought down to a single rate of 73 percent and the 20 percent rate reduced to 17 percent in January 2007. Tariffs on raw material and equipment not produced locally have often been reduced to zero and in 2007, the most of these products are imported duty-free.

Still, the bulk of tariff reduction over the past decade occurred with the framework of preferential agreements, in particular vis-à-vis EU imports.[35] As a result, the average applied most favored nation tariff (24.7 percent) is six times the average EU preferential tariff (4 percent; Figure 2.1).

MFN rates diverge significantly from EU tariffs across sectors and levels of processing. While unilateral cuts into the MFN tariffs have led to a convergence between EU and applied MFN rates on raw materials, gaps remain wide on semi-finished and finished goods (Figure 2.2). While the tariff gap for raw material is about 11 points, those for finished products reach 22.5 points. Between these, semi-finished products face a gap in tariff of 14.5 percentage points, depending on whether they are imported from the EU or GAFTA or from a country with which Tunisia has no preferential agreement. The largest tariff gaps are found in textiles and clothing, leather and footwear, wood, paper and furniture. In Textile and Clothing, the authorities' effort to reduce the cost for all producers has translated in a narrow gap and lower tariffs levied on the industry raw materials. However, the gap on tariffs levied on finished products is high given the high level of applied MFN (12.9 and 40.5 percent respectively). The Tunisian government's believes that EU final products are not as big of a threat to the locally produced. By contrast, they fear that liberalizing imports from cheaper location such as China would hurt the domestic economy and employment.

The large gap between Preferential and MNF tariffs creates a serious challenge for the government. Maintaining this gap may lead to trade diversion while providing an incentive for fraud (especially on the origin of products). At the same time, in contrast with the EU,

---

35. Tariffs on GAFTA imports are zero since 2005 but non-tariff barriers such technical controls are used across GAFTA countries to restrict trade. Authorities in the region argue that this is necessary because of frauds on the origin of products that create unfair competition in the local markets.

Figure 2.1. Average Tariff by Import Regime (2007)

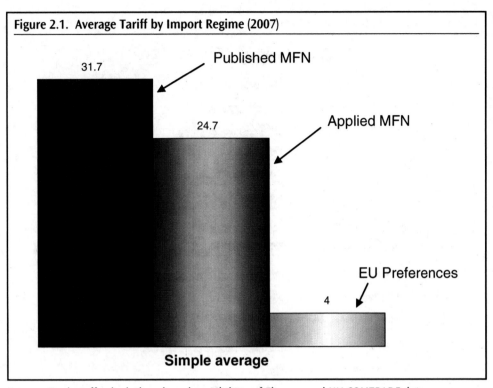

Source: Bank staff calculations based on Ministry of Finance and UN COMTRADE data.

Asian countries (that face the MFN tariffs) have generally lower prices and competitive exchange rates and may pose a more serious threat to Tunisian industries. Today, Tunisia has reached a point where further reductions of tariffs on imports from the EU without reducing tariffs on other import sources would reduce welfare because of trade diversion. Simulations in the next section confirm that the cost of trade diversion now outweighs the welfare benefit of further tariff reductions on EU imports of industrial goods.

Another source of tariff dispersion stems from the large difference between agricultural products and manufactures. Agriculture was considered "sensitive" by both the EU and Tunisia and was shielded from the liberalization process.[36] As a result, tariffs on agricultural products are in the 49–73 percent range, while MFN tariffs on manufactures are mostly 20–30 percent. Thus the protection in agriculture is much higher than in manufacturing (Figure 2.3).[37] Most imported agri-food products are subject to very high customs duties and complex technical regulations, which, for a number of products, have not sufficed to discourage the demand for imports. Tariffs peak apply to 69 percent of agricultural tariff lines and applied rates average 67 percent. Import of many agricultural products is a monopoly

36. The little in the way of liberalization in agriculture consisted of enlarging gradually and bilaterally the quotas on trade of a specified list of products under specific periods, which provides only marginal opportunities in terms of market access.

37. Agriculture generates about 14 percent of GDP and employs about 22 percent of the labor force in Tunisia. Agricultural production has performed well, with yields growing at 2.8 percent per year since 1989, allowing the sector to keep pace with overall economic growth. It provided a quarter of Tunisia's new jobs in the 1990s, creating twice as many jobs per unit of GDP as the economy overall.

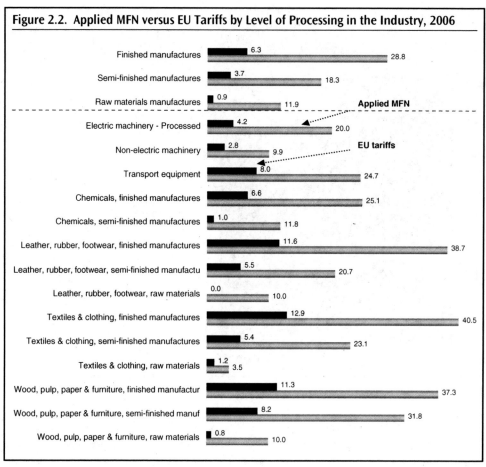

Figure 2.2. Applied MFN versus EU Tariffs by Level of Processing in the Industry, 2006

Category	Applied MFN	EU tariffs
Finished manufactures	6.3	28.8
Semi-finished manufactures	3.7	18.3
Raw materials manufactures	0.9	11.9
Electric machinery - Processed	4.2	20.0
Non-electric machinery	2.8	9.9
Transport equipment	8.0	24.7
Chemicals, finished manufactures	6.6	25.1
Chemicals, semi-finished manufactures	1.0	11.8
Leather, rubber, footwear, finished manufactures	11.6	38.7
Leather, rubber, footwear, semi-finished manufactu	5.5	20.7
Leather, rubber, footwear, raw materials	0.0	10.0
Textiles & clothing, finished manufactures	12.9	40.5
Textiles & clothing, semi-finished manufactures	5.4	23.1
Textiles & clothing, raw materials	1.2	3.5
Wood, pulp, paper & furniture, finished manufactur	11.3	37.3
Wood, pulp, paper & furniture, semi-finished manuf	8.2	31.8
Wood, pulp, paper & furniture, raw materials	0.8	10.0

Source: Bank staff calculations based on Ministry of Finance data.

of the "Office des Céréales" to keep the producer price up and the price to millers down via public subsidies.[38]

The policy dilemma now facing Tunisia is that any further reductions in its tariffs on imports from EU, while reducing the average level of protection, may greatly increase the dispersion in protection—both the dispersion between agriculture and manufacturing, and the dispersion between different country sources of manufactured goods. Since the welfare damage done by import protection comes from the dispersion and well as the average level, Tunisia's current policy course may not yield benefits unless the question of dispersion is also addressed.[39] The extent of this policy dilemma is examined empirically in section 2 to support reform options.

---

38. Tunisian private traders/millers cannot directly tender for wheat destined to be consumed domestically. However, they can import wheat under toll milling and re-exportation arrangements. These arrangements ensure that Tunisian farmers earn much more than the world price for wheat (World Bank 2006).

39. For the empirical analysis, the structure of protection from the GTAP version 6 database is used, since although it slightly overstates the current tariffs on manufactures from the EU, it picks up the incidence of tariff rate quotas and specific tariffs in agriculture, as well as the likely real structure of protection against imports from GAFTA countries.

Figure 2.3.   Tariff Dispersion and Share in Total Import by Tariff Rate, Industry and Agriculture (2006)

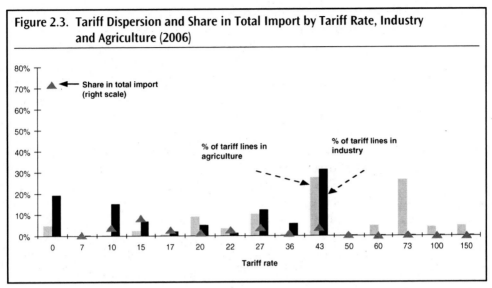

Source: Bank staff calculations based on Ministry of Finance data.

The challenges of implementing Overlapping Preferential Agreements. Tunisia's tariff regime is made even more complex by the coexistence of a large number of overlapping preferential agreements. A part from the EU, Tunisia has signed an FTA with the 18 members of the Arab League under the Greater Arab Free Trade Area (GAFTA), an agreement with Morocco, Egypt and Turkey as a group (AGADIR agreement) and eight other bilateral agreements. Imports from preferential partners entering Tunisia face lower tariffs in general, although non-tariff barriers tend to reduce the take-up of such preferences.

- *There is a duty-free treatment of imports from GAFTA, on paper.* As part of the GAFTA agreement signed in 1998, tariffs of all industrial goods and most agricultural products were being dismantled, and industrial goods face duty-free tariffs across GAFTA countries since 2005. However, most GAFTA members including Tunisia use non-tariff barriers such as technical norms and rules of origin barriers to restrict trade. Consistent reports reveal that importers often select to pay the higher MFN rates because of the high costs of obtaining the preferential treatment. Authorities across GAFTA argue that without the recourse to non-tariff barriers, massive fraud on the origin of imports would lead to unfair competition in the local market.
- *Preferential treatment is also accorded under eight other FTAs.* Tunisia has signed eight bilateral and two pluri-lateral agreements (the AGADIR agreement with Jordan, Morocco and Egypt and the agreement with the EFTA composed of Switzerland, Norway, Island and Liechtenstein) and six bilateral agreements with Morocco, Egypt, Jordan, Syria, Libya, Turkey.[40]

The implementation of the above agreements poses an enormous administrative challenge since they overlap, have different implementation schedules, different product coverage and

---

40. Tunisia has signed a preferential agreement with the European Free Trade Area (Suisse, Norvège, Islande, Liechtenstein) in 2004. This agreement entered into force in 1998. It proposes to replicate the Tunisia-EU AA reciprocal commitments to AFTA countries.

different rules of origin. In particular, difficulties in implementing the 10 free-trade agreements signed by Tunisia arise from:

- The overlapping between bilateral and pluri-lateral agreements such as the GAFTA and AGADIR that include countries with which Tunisia has a bilateral agreement. For instance, the GAFTA overlaps with the bilateral agreements concluded with Morocco, Libya, Egypt, Jordan and Syria. Which provision applies to which product under what circumstance is often hard to determine rapidly.
- The overlapping schedules in completing tariff barriers dismantling. While 2008 is the official completion date of most FTAs (EU, EFTA, Morocco, Egypt, and Jordan), "free trade" with Turkey is delayed until 2014. And while the bilateral FTA with Morocco, Jordan and Egypt is not yet concrete, the complete dismantling of tariffs on imports from GAFTA and AGADIR is theoretically complete since 2005.
- The fact that same products face different tariff dismantling schedules. For instance, while under GAFTA, the tariff faced by a Moroccan industrial product is zero, under the Tunisia-Morocco bilateral free trade agreement, the same product would face 20 percent of the applied MFN rate.
- Different negative lists (products excluded from dismantling) in different agreements.
- Different Rules of Origin. ROO are used to determine whether a good is eligible for preferential treatment such as reduced or zero tariff or not. Under Tunisia's FTAs, a product is said to originate in the free trade area or the preferential partner when it is grown, harvested, wholly produced, or "substantially transformed" in the free trade

area or the partner. Tunisia applies 3 types of ROO depending on the definition of "substantially transformed" (table 2.1). In its agreement with Morocco, Egypt, Jordan, Libya, Syria and GAFTA, substantially transformed means that at least 40 percent of the value-added is realized in the partner country. In the agreements such as AGADIR, Turkey, EFTA, and the EU, detailed, product-specific ROO apply. However, since August 2006, Tunisia applies the Pan-Euro-Med protocol on rules of origin (ROO), which allows a cumulation of origin (counting as local value-added) with the EU, Turkey and EFTA countries.[41] The Pan-Euro-Med protocol allows for instance Tunisian textile exporters to purchase inputs from Turkey and be still eligible to duty-free at entry in the EU (and vice-versa).

Table 2.1. Rules of Origin Applied by Tunisia in its Preferential Agreements

Detailed ROO	EU
	Turkey
	EFTA
	AGADIR
Value-added > 40%	Morocco
	Egypt
	Jordan
	Libya
	Syria
	GAFTA
Euro-Med ROO	EFTA
	Turkey
	AGADIR
	EU

Source: Ministry of Finance, Tunisia.

41. The objective is to make products manufactured from inputs, parts and components purchased in EFTA countries, five western Balkan nations, Turkey and Euro-Med partners eligible for duty-free entry in the Europe.

It is well-established that the complex rules governing preferences and ineffective implementation contribute to a little impact of the agreements signed on integration (World Bank 2005). It is no surprise that some FTAs have little impact on trade since the latter depends upon the design of the agreement (product coverage, rules governing the granting of preferences, the extent of additional policy reform) and the way that it is implemented (World Bank 2007). While the AA with the EU is implemented fully satisfactorily, the implementation of GAFTA suffers from limited confidence in the system and the use of preemptive measures to avoid frauds.

Finally, the pursuit of multiple and overlapping agreements taxes Tunisia's administrative capacity and reduces transparency as it requires negotiation, administration, and maintenance of multiple tariff schedules, with different "special" sectors, exemptions, etc. A decisive move toward simpler ROO applied by all regional partners would go a long way toward advancing regional integration. Available empirical evidence, while limited, supports the view that well-designed and implemented regional trade agreements can generate increased intra-bloc trade with relatively low inefficiency (World Bank 2005).

The dichotomy between offshore and onshore "sectors." The Tunisian authorities have maintained a policy of generous privileges for investments in selected economic activities and for exporting, by supporting the creation of "offshore" firms. Over the years, this strategy has helped address the import substitution bias of Tunisia's trade policy and thus contributed to promoting export-oriented growth. Indeed, export growth in Tunisia has been led almost exclusively by the offshore industry that has benefited from preferential export policies, leaving the onshore industry behind. Now that onshore firms are less protected by high tariffs than in the past, the incentive and regulatory gap between onshore and offshore is more visible and important. Yet, the onshore sector is filled with firms that have the potential to be large exporters if the business environment within which they operate is improved. A more competitive onshore sector can also help strengthen the linkages between the offshore and the onshore sectors.

In fact, the government has taken a series of measures in recent years to reduce the incentive gap between onshore and offshore sectors:

- Trade facilitation measures to reduce transaction costs in the onshore sector (fast registration, reduction in the number of procedures and of customs documents, new system of normalized and simplified documentation for external trade transactions);
- Tariffs on raw materials, equipment and capital goods are now reduced to zero for a large share of onshore firms now, whether the imports originate from a preferential partner or not;
- Export promotion tools are reaching more and more onshore firms (for example, FAMEX), helping reduce market access disadvantage of the latter;
- On December 2006, a fiscal law reduced the onshore corporate tax from 35 to 30 percent, raised the offshore corporate tax from zero to 10 percent, increased VAT reimbursement to 100 percent as of 2008, re-balanced VAT rates (6, 12 and 18 percent) and suppressed the 29 percent rate; and

▓ Finally, offshore firms are now allowed to sell up to 30 percent of their production in the onshore sector and be subject to the onshore fiscal regime on that proportion.

While the above measures go in the right direction, much more is needed to reduce the dichotomy between the offshore and the on-shore regimes. Indeed, in contrast with offshore firms competing mostly in international markets, firms in the onshore sector suffer from many structural constraints, including anti-competitive practices and constraints in both labor and credit markets (IEQ 2006b).

Anti-competitive practices. Tunisia's competition legislation has been upgraded and the power and autonomy of the competition council has been reinforced. Thanks to a 2005 law, the competition council can now trigger legal actions related to anticompetitive practices. However, the improved institutional framework for competition has not yet allowed a significant reduction in anti-competitive practices and unfair competition in the domestic market. A firm-level study by the *Institut d'Economie Quantitative* shows a high prevalence of unfair competition and anticompetitive practices and fiscal evasion (which create a distortion between firms paying normally their taxes or those that do not). About 60 percent of firms operating in the domestic market denounced anti-competitive practices such as implicit agreements, discrimination among clients and linked sales. Regarding unfair competition, 67 percent of firms denounced at least one type of unfair competition in the domestic market. As Table 2.2 shows, overall, the prevalence of all types of unfair competition has increased in all sectors between 2005 and 2006.

Table 2.2. Sectoral Distribution of Firms Decrying Unfair Competition

	Counterfeit (illegal)		Fiscal Evasion		Social Security Contribution Avoidance		Informal Distribution Networks		Other	
	2005	2006	2005	2006	2005	2006	2005	2006	2005	2006
Agribusiness	27	40	33	26	18	23	48	54	15	6
Textiles	33	34	32	49	46	57	18	19	2	11
Chemical	35	43	44	50	25	48	22	57	2	9
IMCCV	26	37	43	53	44	43	30	40	4	7
MEE	29	45	25	36	26	41	16	39	4	6
Diverse	44	47	42	47	40	45	20	41	2	6
Total industry	33	41	34	43	34	45	22	38	4	8

Notes: MEE = Mechanical and electrical engineering; IMCCV = Construction materials.
Source: Enterprise Survey, IEQ 2006.

Rigidity of firing laws. Another major constraint faced by onshore firms is related to the rigidities in the labor legislation emanating from well-meaning social protection objectives. Tunisia has decentralized wage setting schemes (wages and fringe benefits determined in the context of collective agreements within branches and/or within firms), minimum wages have kept pace with productivity (leaving the labor cost constant) and employees can hire individuals on a temporary basis though fixed-term contracts.[42] However, regulations on dismissal procedures remain very rigid in the case of open-ended contracts or CDDs for workers executing open ended activities. Tunisia regulates individual dismissals, as well as collective dismissals due to economic and technical reasons.[43] While international experience shows that flexible rules for collective dismissals due to economic and technical reasons are necessary to allow firms to restructure and improve productivity, in Tunisia, firms (private and public) wanting to downsize must engage in a lengthy bureaucratic process. As a result, temporary unemployment and part-time work have become much more important adjustment mechanisms. While this could be interpreted as a positive trend in the sense of reducing retrenchments, it is not desirable over the long run if necessary restructuring is being avoided.

A related issue is that social security contributions required from firms are deemed too high (49 percent of firms think it is too much according to the IEQ's Enterprise survey). Workers and employers in the private sector contribute the equivalent of 23.75 percent of the wage bill to a social security fund-the employer contribution amounting to 16 percent of gross wages. However, other indirect social charges (such as group insurance, protective clothing, and safety provisions) bring total social charges on labor for employers to 28 percent. Thus, the many small charges add up to a substantial supplementary indirect cost on labor (World Bank, 2003a). Since over 70 percent of the formal non-agricultural labor force is covered by the social security system, it is crucial to evaluate the impact of social charges on job creation. High labor costs may discourage job creation and put Tunisia in a disadvantage to its competitors.

Constraints in the financial sector. Tunisia's onshore firms face poor access to and high priced credit. According to the *Institut d'Economie Quantitative's* recent Competitiveness Report (IEQ 2006), 36 percent of Tunisian firms rate access to credit as a major constraint and 53 percent consider the cost of credit too high. There are two broad views of what determines how much private credit a financial system would extend to firms and individuals.[44] According to the first, formalized by Townsend (1979), Aghion and Bolton (1992), and Hart and Moore (1994, 1998), what matters is the power of creditors. When lenders can easily force repayment or grab collateral, they are more willing to extend credit. According to the second view, pioneered Jaffe and Russell (1976) and Stiglitz and Weiss (1981), what matters for lending is information. When lenders know more about borrowers or their credit history, they are more likely to extend more credit. Using relevant data of 129 countries,

---

42. There are two different situations when temporary contracts can apply. First in the case of activities that are indeed temporary: (i) temporary increase in activity; (ii) replacing a sick employee; (iii) seasonal activities. The second situation refers to open-ended activities. Here temporary contracts can be used for a maximum of 4 years and provide access to the same rights (including social insurance) that workers with open-ended contracts (CDIs) have. The reforms of the labor code also introduced part time work, defined as an activity occupying less than 70 percent of normal working time (World Bank 2007).

43. Like in most countries in the MENA region there are two forms of individual dismissal: (i) serious misdemeanor ("faute grave"), which could include dishonest behavior, sabotage, and considerable disrespectful attitudes; or (ii) without serious misdemeanor. In the first case there is no need for advanced notice and no indemnity is paid. In the second case, the employer first has to discuss the problem (performance, the post is no longer needed), with the employee and try to find a solution. If at the end the employee is dismissed, a period of advanced notice and severance pay apply (see below). An added burden to the employer is that in both cases the employee may go to the court and contest the decision of the employer. If the judge dictates that the employee should be reintegrated, then the employer has to pay the salaries for the time the employee was out of work. The employer can decide not to reintegrate the worker and in this case an indemnity set by the judge has to be paid (for more information, see World Bank 2007).

44. See Djankov, McLiesh and Shleifer (2006) for more details about these two schools of thought.

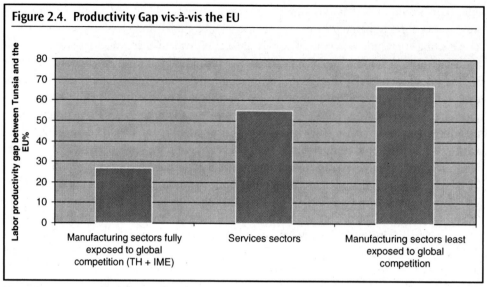

Figure 2.4. Productivity Gap vis-à-vis the EU

Note: Sectors exposed to international trade are textiles and clothing and mechanical and electrical engineering. The other manufacturing sectors are considered as less exposed to international trade.
Source: Bank staff calculation based on Tunisia and OECD data.

Djankov, McLiesh and Shleifer (2006) found that "both creditor protection through the legal system and information sharing institutions are associated with higher ratios of private credit to GDP, but that the former is relatively more important in the richer countries."

In the case of Tunisia, access to information by lenders is a severe constraint which banks compensate through over-collateralization.[45] The amount of collateral requested by banks is as high as 174 percent of the value of credits requested by firms on average and 203 percent for small firms. At the same time, the share of non-performing loans (NPL), inherited from past policies, stands at 20 percent of GDP in 2006, which undermined the capacity of Tunisia's financial sector (now dominated by private banks) to finance investment at low cost is significantly undermined. It is important to note that the offshore firms are served by eight offshore banks operating in a more favorable environment (for more information on Tunisia's banking system, see IMF-World Bank FSAP, 2006).

The aforementioned constraints reduce productivity. As a result of the above constraints and the remaining protection, productivity levels in the onshore sector are much lower than in the offshore sector, indicating that economic growth and income could be higher if those constraints are removed. As Figure 2.4 shows, labor productivity gap vis-à-vis the EU is much higher in the sectors least exposed to international trade. Tunisia's labor productivity in the latter is 73 percent of EU's. In sharp contrast, the average labor productivity in Tunisia's least exposed sectors is only 33 percent of EU's (a gap of 67 percent). Box 2.1 discusses the theoretical channels through which openness affects productivity and growth in the new growth models.

---

45. There are no private credit registries while the public credit bureau (Centrale des Risques), supervised by the Central Bank, is more geared towards avoiding systemic risks. Indeed, loans below US$13,605 are not recorded and access to credit history is limited to the creditors' own customers. It is thus difficult to assign a credit rating to a SME and finance new entrants in the credit market.

Removing the constraints faced by onshore firms could also help boost private investment ratios, which have been sluggish in recent years (12-13 percent of GDP). Breaking down private investment by the origin of the invested funds, it appears that the weakness in private investment is driven by domestic private investment, not FDI (Figure 2.5). Over the period 1996–2007, if total private investment has been dynamic in the energy, mining, real estate and mechanical and electrical engineering sectors, it has declined in tourism, textiles and clothing, agriculture, and fisheries, and has been sluggish in agro-industries and chemicals (Diop 2008). In any case, Tunisia's investment performance pales compared to East European competitors (18-19 percent in Bulgaria and Romania), fast-growing East Asian countries (28-30 percent),[46] and many MENA countries (Morocco 25 percent in 2007).[47]

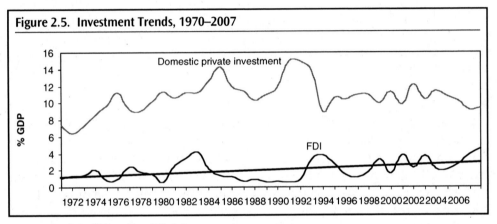

Figure 2.5. Investment Trends, 1970–2007

Source: Bank Staff based on INS data.

Tunisia's Increasingly Challenged Competitive Position in the Euro-Med Space

Regional Competitors for FDI are catching up fast . . . Tunisia's attractiveness lies in its proximity to the world's largest market (the EU), its macro stability, its good human capital base, and its security. Furthermore, the Government has deployed various reforms and strategies to attract FDI as seen in Chapter 1. These approaches include: (i) providing generous fiscal incentives to exporting firms in the area of taxation, the labor regime and the rules for foreign trade as seen above; (ii) improving domestic infrastructure; (iii) promoting skills development to meet the needs of investors' and labor raise productivity; (iv) establishing a dedicated FDI promotion agency (FIPA) and; (v) improving the regulatory environment.

Tunisia has successfully used the above "factors" to attract FDI in a context where reforms in the other countries of the Maghreb were lackluster. Indeed, when it comes to attracting FDI, Tunisia was far behind Bulgaria and Romania in the late 1990s, but was a star performer within the Maghreb region (Figure 2.6). Since 2000 however, countries of the region are catching up fast (Figure 2.7). While the share of FDI in GDP increased by 15 percent in Tunisia, it has doubled in Algeria, quadrupled in Turkey and rose almost 10-fold in Morocco.

---

46. Private gross capital formation increased at an average annual rate of 8.9 percent in Malaysia and 7.6 percent in Thailand after 1965.

47. Private investment averaged 20 percent in Morocco in 2001–05.

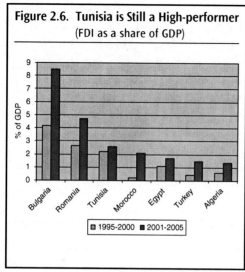

Figure 2.6. **Tunisia is Still a High-performer** (FDI as a share of GDP)

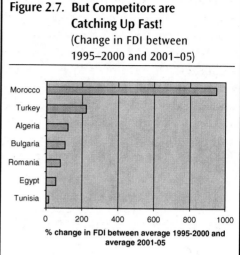

Figure 2.7. **But Competitors are Catching Up Fast!** (Change in FDI between 1995–2000 and 2001–05)

Source: World Bank, WDI.

Clearly, if Tunisia does not implement some strategic positioning policies soon, current trends may continue and Morocco and Egypt will overtake Tunisia in the next few years. Further improving the positioning of the country in the Euro-Med area and increasing the flow of foreign direct investments flowing to Tunisia's industries is thus a priority. What are at stake are not only greater investments and possibilities of job creation but also the ability to tap into global knowledge and new technologies that come with FDI. Knowledge and technologies are also now key drivers of competitiveness, making it important to attract FDI from countries closer to the technology frontier (see Box 2.1).

Logistics services are good but can be further improved. The Logistics Performance Index (LPI), recently developed by the World Bank (see www.worldbank.org/lpi), can help in analyzing different aspects of the global logistics performance and identifying areas of strengths and weaknesses. As Figure 2.8 shows, Tunisia has among the best logistics indicators in the region but lags behind Turkey and Eastern European countries which have benefited from regulatory convergence and institutional twinning with Europe in recent years.

Tunisia is ranked 60th among the 150 countries in the LPI. It ranks within the 10 best performers among the lower middle income group, thanks to its performance on customs, infrastructure, and domestic logistics costs (World Bank 2007d). However, Tunisia faces several constraints related to the limited availability of modern logistics platforms and warehouses. Exporters are small and often cannot by themselves fill a whole container, putting the onus on the efficiency of grouping and coordination by the logistics providers. Unfortunately, the latter are small and atomized and have not been able to minimize coordination failures. Often, grouping of transportation is undertook once or twice a weak, occasioning delays. Opportunities of gaining economies of scale and reducing costs are therefore missed.

Box 2.1. How Can FDI Enhance Technological Development?

Attracting FDI is, along with import of equipment and technology purchases and licensing, theoretically a crucial way to tap into global knowledge and facilitate technological change and productivity growth (See Hoekman and Javorcik 2007 for a comprehensive analysis). In reality, a key question is whether FDI inflows generate vertical spillover effects (as in the case of vertical trade integration between the sectors of two country) and/or horizontal spillover effects within an industry (Hoekman and Javorcik 2007). More specifically, do multinationals have the incentives to deliberately transfer technologies to upstream local firms in developing countries that supply intermediate inputs, parts or components and under what conditions? And is horizontal spillover happening?

The evidence on FDI externalities is that vertical spillovers are much more likely to take place than horizontal spillovers. Foreign firms are keen to transfer technology to their local suppliers because they have a vested interest in having good quality parts, components and intermediate inputs at the lowest cost possible. However, the process is not automatic. For instance, Blomström and Kokko (2003) show that the expected spillovers used to justify the provision of incentives only take place if the domestic firms are sufficiently capable. Analyzing evidence on spillovers, their research concludes that domestic sector efficiency improvements should accompany any FDI incentives. There are many examples of such accompanying policies implemented around the world. For instance, in Czech Republic, the government has put in place a program consisting of evaluating, through consultants, the areas of the business operations of promising SME that need to be improved in order to maximize their chance of being selected as a supplier (Djankov and Hoekman 2007). Similar programs exist also in Ireland and other countries.

The policy implication is therefore to promote vertical integration with global production network. Tunisia has already a large experience on this, in fact the two largest sectors in the manufacturing sector in terms of employment (textiles, and Mechanical and Electrical Engineering) operate largely under this mode. There are however scope to generalize this business model to most other sectors in the economy.

As a result of the above weaknesses, *total* logistics costs (transport, storage, delay, administration) are high in Tunisia. For instance, the logistics costs (freight, administration of logistics, storage, etc.) are estimated to be as high as 17 percent on average in the pharmaceutical and chemical industries. They reach 12 percent in many industries and in the distribution sector, and 10 percent in the agro-industry (Table 2.3). Although logistics costs are lowest in the automobile sector, some firms in the electrical wiring segment, where Tunisia is a leading exporter, have reportedly lost orders because of logistics problems. Limited warehouses and poor logistics services are also an impediment to the development of modern distribution networks.

Looking forward, Tunisia needs to anticipate another potential integration challenge: the growth in cargo traffic in the Mediterranean Sea. It is estimated that maritime traffic will increase by an average 9 percent annually by 2015 (see Figure 2.9). Without a deep-water port to accommodate large shippers, Tunisia will be mostly served by feeders from major ports in the Euro-Med area. As suggested by the example of Tangier, transshipment port will increase the global connectivity of Tunisia, lower cost and delays to access non-EU markets, enhance the quality of services, and develop new activities. Investment in a deep-water port would also allow Tunisia to trade directly with Asian countries and cut costs.

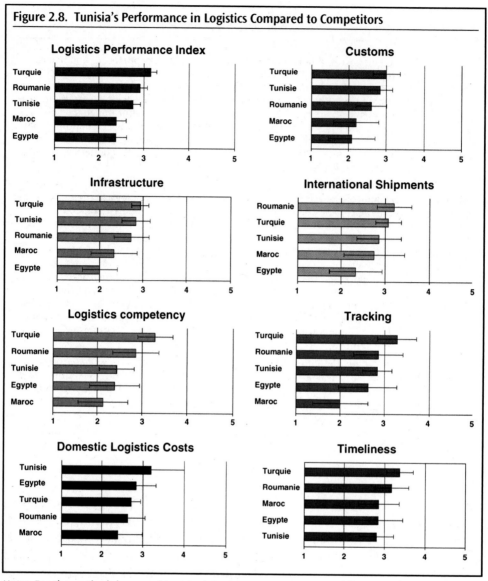

Figure 2.8. Tunisia's Performance in Logistics Compared to Competitors

Note: For the methodology used to calculate the score, see www.worldbank.org/lpi.
Source: World Bank, Database on logistics services.

Innovation and technological development need to be enhanced. The competitive positioning of Tunisia in the Euro-Med area will be increasingly influenced by the country's technological absorption and innovation capacities. Indeed, global firms seek to collaborate with firms that have the capacity to rapidly absorb global technology and adapt rapidly. The enhanced global integration of Tunisia's manufacturing sector itself can provide an important boost to technological development in the country as less protected firms have a stronger incentive to invest and innovate than protected ones (see below). But if macro factors such as trade liberalization and macro stability are important (Lederman 2007), they are not enough. Investment in specific skills and in research and development (R&D),

Table 2.3. Logistics Costs in Percentage of Sales	
Sector	% of Total Sales
Chemicals, pharmaceuticals and cosmetics	17%
Products of mass consumption	13%
Distribution	12%
Other industries	12%
Construction and civil works	11%
Agri-business	10%
Automobile	8%

Source: World Bank estimates (Transport and Logistics Technical Assistance).

purchase of patents, and firm-to-firm and firm-to-university collaboration (externalization and intensification) are key to enhance firm's absorptive and innovation capacities (Lederman 2007; De Ferranti 2003). The policy and institutional framework for raising technology and innovation capacities should ensure an effective interconnectivity and collaboration of all players with the least bureaucracy possible.

Tunisia has an elaborate system of innovation and technical support to firms, including a Higher Council for Scientific Research and Technology to set policy options, technopoles to promote industrial clustering and densification, sectoral technical centers to provide technical support to firms in eight sectors (compliance with technical norms, diffusion of knowledge, etc.), industrial upgrading programs *"mise a niveau"* (PMN, PMI) to assist in material and immaterial investment and improvement of organizational, technological, and marketing capabilities, and a network of laboratories. This support system is geared toward assisting Tunisian firms, predominantly small and with limited capacities to invest significantly in innovation.

To gauge the effectiveness of Tunisia's innovation system, Table 2.4 benchmarks Tunisia against Morocco, Egypt, Romania and Korea focusing on drivers of innovation, which the above institutions try to influence. Tunisia is clearly among the best performers in the Euro-Med area but is a long way from the performance of countries like Korea. Relative to the region, its strengths lie in the country's enrollment rate in Science and Technology fields, its

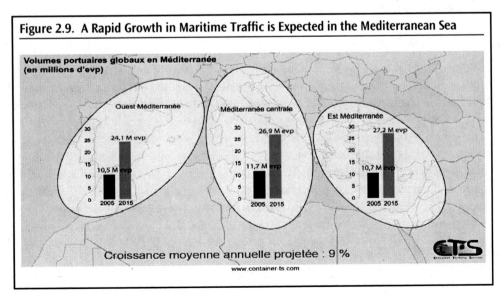

Figure 2.9. A Rapid Growth in Maritime Traffic is Expected in the Mediterranean Sea

Source: World Bank estimates (Transport and Logistics Technical Assistance).

number of researchers in R&D, and its participation to global value chains (which enhances vertical technological spillovers). Compared to Korea, Morocco and Eastern European countries however, Tunisian firms undertake less direct purchase of technology and have a lower penetration of Information Technology (IT). Another area of weakness is the limited collaboration between the universities and businesses on research and their application.

Table 2.4. Benchmarking Tunisia on Key Determinants of Innovation

Variable	Tunisia	Egypt	Morocco	Romania	Korea
Science and Engineering Enrolment Ratio (%), 2005	30.90	n/a	21.20	25.00	39.90
Scientific and Technical Journal Articles/Mil. People, 2003	46.12	24.12	14.86	45.53	287.57
Researchers in R&D/Mil. People, 2004	1013	n/a	n/a	976	3187
Total Expenditure for R&D as % of GDP, 2004	0.63	0.19	0.62	0.4	2.6
Private Sector Spending on R&D (1–7), 2006	3.7	2.7	3	3.1	5.1
University-Company Research Collaboration (1–7), 2006	3.7	2.6	3	2.9	4.6
Firm-Level Technology Absorption (1–7), 2006	5.2	4.7	5	4.6	5.9
Royalty and License Fees Payments (US$/pop.), 2005	0.81	2.50	1.50	8.00	91.10
Royalty and License Fees Receipts (US$/pop.), 2005	1.40	1.80	0.40	2.20	37.80
High-Tech Exports as % of Manuf. Exports, 2005	4.9	0.6	10.1	3.4	32.30
Value Chain Presence (1–7), 2006	4.7	4	3.4	3.3	5.5

Note: See annex 2 for the definition of variables and corresponding spider diagrams.
Source: World Bank Knowledge Assessment Methodology (KAM) (www.worldbank.org/kam).

Results in Table 2.4 are consistent with recent findings of enterprise surveys which provide more qualitative information. For instance, in the IEQ's 2006 enterprise survey, 40 percent of firms declare having invested in R&D to add value to their products.[48] However, 86 percent of those firms undertake R&D within their firm; only 20 percent of firms collaborate with the "technopoles" in R&D and only 15 percent collaborate with universities. As regards ICT, while almost all large firms have Internet connection, only 62 percent of small firms (the majority of firms in Tunisia) declare being connected. In terms of quality control and enhancement, 77 percent of firms declare having a quality control unit. Above this average are firms in the chemical industry for technical and normative reasons (compliance to international norms) and firms strongly exposed to global competition such as in textiles,

---

48. The sectoral distribution of responses is as follows: 55 percent for agri-business, 48 percent for textiles and clothing, 43 percent for chemical, 37 percent for construction materials, 30 percent for mechanical and electrical engineering and 28 percent for the "other" industries (IEQ 2006b).

mechanical and electrical engineering and agro-industry. Below the average are firms long shielded from global competition and domestic market-focused (construction materials and "other industries"). Finally, the heaviness of the "bureaucracy" involved in obtaining the services of the various institutions of the innovation system is decried.

Enterprise surveys in Tunisia clearly show that firms exposed to global competition, investing in R&D and control quality units, enjoying good connectivity with the outside world (through good Internet connectivity) and being subject to ex-ante client quality control as in the case of textiles and clothing and mechanical and electrical engineering are able to innovate, move up the value chain, and maintain competitiveness. Indeed, if on average 57 percent of firms declare having created 18 new products on average over the last 5 years, the percentage is 81 percent for firms having invested in R&D. The same conclusion applies to firms moving up the value chain (IEQ 2006b). In all sectors however, small suppliers, with smaller volume orders, often do not invest in R&D and do not have well-developed quality control processes and they lag in product quality and consistency.

Box 2.2. Trade and Innovation in New Growth Models

The hypothesis of constant returns to scale forced the traditional models to postulate that growth rate of technology (or technological development) was exogenous. Indeed, with constant returns to scale and perfect competition (factors remunerated at their marginal productivity) there are no incentives to expand their activities, including through export development (Warsh 2006). Exogenous growth of technical progress was the only path to permanent growth. New growth models rehabilitate the role of entrepreneurs and attempt to demonstrate that entrepreneurs do get some economic rewards when they innovate. That is why around 60 percent of export growth seems to take place through new product varieties, rather than exporting higher volumes of the same goods as found by recent research such as Hummels and Klenow (2005) for large exporters.

In the new growth models, investment in innovation such as R&D helps generate new ideas and processes which ultimately allow production of new varieties or implementation of new production processes. Thus while innovation is costly, it produces economic rewards such as new ideas which entail positive externalities even if they can be patented or copyrighted.[49] Many versions of endogenous growth models emphasize education as a precondition for absorbing new ideas and show that the availability of high quality and abundant human capital permits to avoid diminishing returns (Lucas 1988). In other words, when entrepreneurs innovate, countries can grow permanently in spite of diminishing returns to capital and labor.

The link with trade is straightforward: competition, openness and deregulation and all policies that facilitate new entry put pressure on the entrepreneurs to invest and innovate to remain competitive. The literature distinguishes between frontier firms and catch-up firms. The former are leaders in their business, enjoy economic rents and have little incentive to invest unless they become concerned about new entrants threatening their position. For catch-up firms, either the lure of extra profit motivate them to invest in innovation or their distance to the local market frontier technology is so long and their ability to mobilize finance so limited that they likely exit the market (Aghion and Hawitt 2006). Many policy implications can be derived. For instance, removing barriers to entry and competition is crucial to promote innovation. Facilitating investment in innovation by promising catch-up firms is also important. Improving access to finance, strengthening national innovation systems, and putting in place industrial upgrading programs (such as the *Mise a Niveau* program in Tunisia) are all tools that can help.

---

49.   This is because new ideas can be used to generate other new ideas that can lead to innovation.

Needed Reforms

Simplify the Tariff Regime and Deepen Trade Agreements

Reduce tariff gaps. A way in which Tunisia could address the issue of dispersion in protection is by accompanying the elimination of the remaining tariffs on manufactures from Europe with a concomitant reduction in applied tariffs on imports from other sources. Tariffs on imports from the EU are to be eliminated in the next few years—Tunisia could consider reducing its tariffs on imports from all other sources by 25 percent over the same period. What would be the impact?

Using a four-region FTAP model (Tunisia, the EU, GAFTA and the Rest of the World), the risk of trade diversion has been assessed.[50] The results confirm that manufacturing tariffs against EU imports are now sufficiently low, relative to protection elsewhere, that the welfare cost of exacerbating the dispersion in protection now dominates—phasing out the remaining tariffs against EU manufactures would mean economic well-being was US $184 million per year lower than otherwise, after about ten years. Further liberalization of tariff vis-à-vis the EU without reducing tariffs from other sources would have an adverse effect on welfare.

This adverse effect could be partially offset by reducing tariffs on imports from all other sources by 25 percent. By itself, this would provide gains of US$74 million per year, gains driven by consumer surplus. The combined package of reforms to manufacturing tariffs would yield a net loss of US $104 million per year after about ten years. Yet, the structure of protection in Tunisia is now so variable that perhaps the only strategy in manufacturing to guarantee an overall net gain would be an across-the-board-approach—full liberalization of protection on imports from all sources, both EU and otherwise (which could produce net gains of US$65 million per year after about ten years).

Our simulations show that the worst affected sectors—wood and paper products, metals and products, and transport equipment—would be smaller than otherwise by 10 percent or less after about ten years as a result of eliminating the remaining tariffs on EU imports and cutting tariffs on imports from other sources by 25 percent. The reforms to protection in agriculture and manufacturing would also bring a significant boost to Tunisia's overall trade performance. The reforms in manufacturing would boost aggregate export volumes by 27 percent a year, after about ten years. The sectoral breakdown of exports shows that the improved export performance does not just come from the exportable sectors (Appendix E). Even when import competing sectors contract in response to tariff cuts, the production units that remain are more competitive, and can also improve their export performance, albeit sometimes from a very low base.

In summary, there is now an urgent need to address the increasing dispersion in tariffs created by the gap between tariffs on imports from the EU and imports from other sources. The gap of 11 points in tariffs between these two sources for raw material can be eliminated altogether to enhance firm competitiveness. Furthermore, accompanying the elimination of the remaining tariffs on EU final products with a reduction in tariff rates from other sources appears to be a precondition for further economic gains. These expanded reforms in manufacturing will create adjustment pressures, but they are of a scope to be easily absorbed with normal rates of underlying economic growth and with appropriate social adjustment mechanisms.

---

50. See Appendix C for a detailed description of the FTAP model developed by Dee and Hanslow (2001).

Deepen and harmonize trade agreements. Among the numerous trade agreements signed by Tunisia, the AA with the EU is the only one implemented without major administrative challenges. The limited impact of the other trade agreements is partly due to ineffective implementation, which in turn reflects the lack of coherence and harmony between pluri-lateral and bilateral agreements. The numerous discrepancies (product coverage, rules governing the granting of preferences, the negative lists, etc.) in the provisions of GAFTA versus bilateral agreements with individual GAFTA countries are an illustration of this (see above). The benefits of the AA with the EU would also be ripped fully only with an effective expansion of bilateral liberalization efforts to agriculture and services.

Tunisia should therefore: (i) submit any future preferential agreement to an examination of its harmony with the existing PTAs, to ensure effectiveness and reduce transaction costs and (ii) seek to harmonize the ROO in the existing PTA. In particular, the Pan-Euro Med ROO can be used as a model in modifying/renegotiating ROO is bilateral PTAs; (iii) step up efforts aimed at reciprocally liberalizing agriculture and services.

Further Reduce the Incentive Gap Between the Offshore and Onshore Sectors

Reduce anti-competitive practices. This could necessitate actions at many levels. First, while the legislative texts and the institutional structures are being brought in line with international best practices, enforcement problems remain.

It is necessary to (i) better advertise the new competition legislation through outreach campaigns; (ii) provide the Competition Council with more power (especially the political power to exercise its increased legal power); (iii) increase its human resources (specialized lawyers, economists, accountants) and (iv) amend the law to make it mandatory, not optional, for the government to consult the Council on matters related to competition. Second, anti-competitive practices are in principle responsive to changes in incentives so that reforms aimed at reducing tariffs and taxation of the onshore sector could help.

Reduce the rigidity of the labor market. International experience and Tunisia's situa-tion shows that job protection is associated with lower formal employment and the pro-liferation of part-time and informal jobs. Job protection can also reduce labor mobility and negatively affect labor productivity and overall economic growth.

Thus Tunisia could thus (i) provide less protection within the firm and offer more effective protection outside the firm. This would call for social safety nets that go beyond the very limited aide sociale now in place and well-targeted active labor market programs; (ii) increase flexibility in the rules and procedures governing retrenchments. This would facilitate enterprise restructuring, as overall retrenchment levels are extremely low in Tunisia. Taking steps toward providing less employment protection within the firm and offering more effective protection outside the firm.

Improve onshore firms' access to credit. Improving access to credit is a complex issue that requires sustained actions on both the supply and demand sides. Tunisia's IMF-World Bank Financial Sector Assessment Program (FSAP) Update has identified a number of recommendations, which are still largely valid (IMF 2006).

In line with the FSAP, the government has been improving information on the quality of borrowers by improving the design of the public credit registry and promoting the cre-ation of well-regulated private credit registries; a plan to reduce the nonperforming loans

(NPLs) of the banking system is also being implementing. Moreover, the government is encouraging the provisioning of nonperforming loans (the ratio today is 46.4 percent, against 59 percent for Morocco and 88 percent for Turkey). The 2006 Budget Law has made provisioning fully tax deductible, up from 85 percent in 2005. Further, a May 2006 Law gave the Central Bank new powers to monitor the financial system, ensure alignment with prudential norms and regulations, enforce transparency, and supervise publication of financial and economic data. Building on the important progress in the last two years, the pursuit of the main recommendations of the FSAP could help ease access to credit by onshore firms in the medium term.

Improve Positioning in the Euro-Med Space

Improve trade logistics services. Reforms and investment should help better integration of Tunisian services with international logistics networks, by blending openness and consolidation of local providers. Fortunately, in Tunisia's 11th development plan, an absolute priority is given to transport and logistics infrastructures. In light of the above analysis, the following priority reforms are warranted:

- *Reduce entry barriers and informality in the logistics sector.* Entry in the logistics sector is subject to a "cahier des charges" and a limit on foreign capital ownership to 49 percent maximum. These "entry barriers" reduce private investments in the sector and its modernization. Moreover, small formal SMEs are subject to an unfair competition from the informal sector seriously hampering their exposure of the sector to international best practices, private investment and modernization efforts; So reform options include (i) making sure that the cahier des charges does not unintentionally not go beyond ensure minimum quality standards; (ii) eliminating the limit in the foreign majority ownership and; reducing informality.
- *Encourage investment in modern warehouses and logistics platforms* to allow investors to optimize the management of trade flows and stay competitive in time-sensitive sectors such as textiles and clothing and mechanical and electrical engineering. The government plans to establish or facilitate the development of logistical platforms. The PPP arrangement for such investment (concession, BOT) should better take in account international standards in the area, so as to facilitate investment or co-investment by major international operators. The competitiveness of Tunisia's largest exporting industries—textiles and clothing and mechanical and electrical engineering—hinges on a swift implementation of such policy.
- *Deepen the current trade facilitation efforts.* While some existing measures like TTN have increased the efficiency of international transactions, the port performance can be further improved (about 10 days). Tunisia's port management needs more automation, a streamlining of procedures, and a greater involvement of private operators.[51]

---

51. However, some of the problems are tied to the constraints imposed by the infrastructure like in Radès (obsolete platform for containers, piers that cannot support modern handling equipments, their layout are not compatible with the trend in traffic, Ro-Ro and containers are mixed), OMPP has projects to improve this.

▨ *Invest in deep water ports to reduce the costs of trading with distant markets.* The government has announced the future construction of a deep-water port at Enfhida. Such infrastructure is crucial to maintain the attractiveness of Tunisia for investors. However the benefit of such investment, independently of other considerations (costs, environmental impact), cannot be reaped without substantial improvement in the environment of logistics operations and services.

Enhance domestic innovation and global technological absorption. Over the near term, technological deepening will depend on accelerating the pace of absorption and assimilation by the business sector. Much of applied research and development to assimilate technology needs to be done by firms themselves (which can also guide their proactive search for technology from other sources) and this can be stimulated by more focused government support.

▨ *Improve the relevance of research.* Tunisia has many players in the "innovation" arena, but none of them has the responsibility of assisting in identifying findings of relevance to industry and transferring knowledge from researchers to firms. Given that content of the research will affect the innovativeness of existing industries and the emergence of new industries, an important question is whether the allocation of R&D resources (across disciplines and among sectors) is consistent with what are the perceived as longer term industrial priorities.

▨ *Further strengthen firm-technopole and firm-university collaboration.* A key result from enterprise surveys is that only 20 percent of firms collaborate with the "technopoles" in R&D and only 15 percent collaborate with universities. While industrial clustering is well advanced in Tunisia, an attempt to attract international brand "names" in the technopoles and competitiveness poles could help strengthen collaboration of firms with universities and technopoles. It is well-established that the presence of large firms helps foster a strong relationship between the above actors. A more aggressive advertisement campaign is thus necessary.

▨ *Pro-actively foster partnership between Tunisia's innovation institutions and firms and their European counterparts.* For public institution, the twinning mechanism of the European Union can be a suitable tool to transfer know-how on how to promote innovation.

▨ *Promote ICT diffusion targeting small firms.* While programs such as the *Mise a Niveau* can help, the weakness in ICT indicators is related to the state of competition in the telecom sector. While the mobile sector is open and has expanded tremendously in recent years, the fixed segment is still under a public-private monopoly. As a result, high-speed Internet is still quite expensive in Tunisia.

▨ *Reduce bureaucracy in the innovation system.* Tunisia has a number of actors in the innovation system and procedures to benefit from public sectors' services are time-consuming and complex. With the availability of a large number of private consulting firms, many public entities may become irrelevant if their procedures are not simplified.

CHAPTER 3

Integration Challenges and Reform Options in the Services Markets

While addressing the priority integration issues in the goods sector is likely to contribute to growth in the long run, the bulk of productivity (thus competitiveness) gains and economic expansion in the years ahead will occur in services. In this report, we distinguish two categories of services, even if the distinction is not fully clear-cut. The first category concerns "backbone services" such as telecommunication, banking, transport, and professional services. These services are, *inter alia*, inputs in the production process of firms in all sectors and thus directly affect firm productivity and efficiency. At the same time, they intermediate transactions and can facilitate or hinder the structural transformation of the Tunisian economy. The second category of services encompasses a large number of activities such as engineering, health services and "services to firms" such as accounting, legal services, and ICT for which Tunisia has demonstrated a real export potential in recent years. These new "exportable services" hold high hopes for the development of exports and the creation of jobs, especially for university graduates. The present chapter deals with "backbone services" while the next chapter looks at the newly exportable services.

This chapter undertakes an in-depth regulatory diagnostic for each sector and highlights the key restrictions whose removal may help reduce prices of backbone services. The extent to which prices can be reduced by reforms is estimated. It then examines the potential economy-wide effects of further liberalization of services. Appendix B discusses in depth the different approaches to measuring policy restrictions in services markets.

Where Does Tunisia Stand In Opening Its Services Sectors?

The Government of Tunisia has undertaken a gradual opening of backbone services sectors to private competition. The approach taken has so far been mainly autonomous (as opposed to WTO-focused), with the main objective of improving the economy's competitiveness.

Tunisia has today no free trade agreement (FTA) that includes services. Multilateral liber-alization of services under WTO's GATS has been very limited (for information on the GATS approach to measuring restrictions to services delivery, please refer to Appendix B). Tunisia has only included three sectors (tourism, telecom, and financial sectors) in the (previous) GATS Uruguay Round (UR).[52] While some of the sectors not included are quite open (for example, maritime transport), entry into many services sectors is restricted. For instance, all trading activities, including wholesale distribution and retail trading services, are reserved for enterprises in which Tunisians hold a majority interest. Similarly, for-eigners can hold only a minority interest in building enterprises. For some services activities, foreign investment requires the prior agreement of the *Commission Supérieur des Investissements* (CSI—Investment Commission) if the foreign participation exceeds 50 percent of the company capital (for example, in insurance). Finally, the measures affecting the presence of natural persons (Mode 4) remain unbound, with the exception of wholly exporting enterprises that can recruit up to four executives and managers of foreign nationality.

In its UR schedule of commitments, Tunisia has bound without limitation many mode 1 transactions (for example, in the financial sector), but in reality, those GATS measures overlap with strict foreign exchange controls, making them partly ineffective. Apart from the financing of current operations, opportunities for cross-border trade (Mode 1) are sharply restricted, and foreign competition is mostly possible through commercial presence (Mode 3) or through the presence of natural persons (Mode 4).

It is not clear whether Tunisia will significantly increase its commitments at the end of the ongoing Doha Round. In its *conditional* Doha offer (2005), Tunisia maintained some restrictive horizontal commitments. For instance, under the latter, freedom of investment is guaranteed only to "wholly exporting" firms and a nationality condition is attached to the exercise of commercial activities (whole and retail trade) in Tunisia. In terms of sectoral coverage, five sectors were included in the conditional offer (out of 11 possible): telecom, environmental services, financial services, health services, and tourism and travel.[53] Some important opening reforms are planned in telecom, with the attribution of new licenses in mobile and fixed telephony as well as VSAT. In contrast, the conditional offer in the financial sector is judged limited by some WTO members such as the EU. For instance, insurance companies still need to partner with local firms in order to operate in Tunisia while the general manager of a financial institution, as well as insurance and stock exchange agents and intermediaries, have to hold a Tunisian nationality.

Beside trade negotiations under GATS, Tunisia has started a process of negotiations for a services trade agreement with the EU in March 2006 under the Euro-med context.

---

52. Including sectors in a GATS schedule does not necessarily mean an "opening" of such sectors. Rather, the Government discloses the conditions for entry and doing business in the sector and "bind" them (agree not to change the rules of the game) to send a signal of stability (reduced uncertainty) to investors. However, it is customary to leave sectors, which one does not intend to open out of the schedule.

53. Environment services relate to the management of solid waste, dangerous waste and sanitation. Foreign firms can enter the market but face a majority holding restriction (they can own up to 49% of the capital) and they should agree to transfer technologies, recruit local staff and train staff locally. In the health sector, establishment is free without limit imposed on the capital for a list of medical fields where Tunisia has an export potential.

Discussions of the general provisions of the agreements have started. These will be followed by bilateral negotiations on market access commitments (which services are to be included and what degree of openness). The EU has proposed putting the future agreements in the context of the European Neighborhood Policy and to use some of the implementation tools of this initiative, chiefly regulatory convergence, in some sectors. For Tunisia, mode 4 (temporary movement of professional services providers) and mode 2 in the area of health services represent two big areas of interest. These negotiations are crucial to secure better market access for its services providers to Europe, which would require a relaxing of restrictions in obtaining visas and mutual recognition agreements for diplomas and professional qualifications with some EU countries. On the other hand, greater "portability" of health insurance would help boost exports of Tunisia's health services. Tunisia is less interested in mode 3 (commercial presence) given its limited number of multinationals and in mode 1 (consumption abroad) given the prevalence of capital controls which hinder service provision under this mode.

Sector-by-sector Analysis and Reform Options

Barriers in services trade vary however by sector and a sector-by-sector analysis is needed to identify policy restrictions to entry and competition in services. Box 3.1 provides some details on the collection of qualitative information on regulation and their conversion into indices of restrictiveness in the case of Tunisia.

The Telecom Sector

A Telecommunications are an essential channel of transmission of knowledge, information and technology and are thus crucial for productivity and growth. Further, with the ongoing global fragmentation of services production, further improving the quality of telecommunication services is a key factor in Tunisia's ability to attract off-shoring of services. Pro-competitive reforms in this sector are therefore crucial.

Recent Reforms and Current Market Structure. Until 1996, telecommunications and postal services in Tunisia were provided and regulated by the ministry in charge of postal and telecommunication. In 1996, postal and telecom services were separated, and Tunisie Telecom (TT) was created as the state monopoly for telecom. The new telecom provider soon made important investments to build a GSM network and started providing mobile services in 1998 (Tunicell). In 2001 a new "Code des Communications" authorized the licensing of private operators. This law ascertained the citizen's right to choose his operator, defined licensing requirements and provided a legal basis for the creation of the Tunisian NRA, called INT, created soon afterwards. With a solid legal basis for competition put in place, the Tenth Economic and Social Development Plan (2002–06) called for important investments (about 2.8 billion dinars) for the extension of the fixed and mobile telephone network, the modernization of the data transmission networks, and an increase in telephone density. The plan recommended that approximately 40 percent of the investment should be made by the private sector. These developments led to issuance of a new mobile license in 2002, granted to a private mobile operator, Orascom, and later another

---

Box 3.1. Methodology for Measuring Restrictions Affecting Services Delivery

---

The approach taken in this report consists of measuring restrictions based on "regulation" questionnaires developed by the OECD and the Productivity Commission of Australia that attempt to capture all the regulations that can affect significantly entry, competition and trade in services.[54] The questionnaires have been submitted to Tunisia's regulators, administration and private sector in order to collect qualitative information on entry, competition and business conduct barriers in the following services sectors: banking, insurance, telecommunications, air transport, accounting, legal and engineering services.

The first step is to quantify the extent of current barriers. To measure services restrictions we collected qualitative information about regulatory restrictions affecting services delivery in Tunisia and converted it into a quantitative index (or indexes), using weights that reflect the relative severity of the different restrictions. The general approach in Findlay and Warren, used here, is to convert qualitative information about regulatory restrictions into a quantitative index, using a priori judgments about the relative restrictiveness of different barriers (i.e., the weighs of the restrictiveness index components). This is generally less contentious within a given category of barrier than between. For example, it makes sense to score a regime that restricts foreign ownership to 25 percent or less as being twice as restrictive as one that restricts foreign ownership to 50 percent or less. What is less obvious is how to weight the scores on foreign ownership restrictions together with those on licensing requirements, or those on restrictions on lines of business. Nevertheless, some of the inherent arbitrariness of the weighting procedures can be tested empirically.

One rich source of index measures, providing a benchmark reference, is the OECD studies of product market regulation (OECD 2005a, 2005b). We use OECD questionnaires to quantify the market entry and business restrictions in air passenger transport and the accounting, legal and engineering professions. The benchmarking of Tunisia in these sectors is thus done against OECD countries. However, since the OECD questionnaires do not distinguish whether the restrictions affect only foreign operators or also affect domestic players, it is not sensible to use them for sectors such as banking where discriminatory restrictions are often rife. Here for banking and telecommunication, we employ the restrictiveness index developed by Australian Productivity Commission (APC), which captures a measure of discrimination against foreigners—limitations on national treatment. The APC restrictiveness indexes are also used for telecom because the OECD questionnaire gives too much weight to the share of the services providers in the market, whereas Tunisia's recent reforms are too new to induce the new providers to secure a large share in the market.

Once restrictiveness indices consistent with those generated by OECD and APC are constructed for the different sectors, the second stage is to quantify the effects of these indexes of services trade barriers on some behind-the-border measure of economic performance—here prices or price-cost margins—while controlling for all the other factors that affect prices of services in that market. These econometric results are used to construct the counterfactual—what prices would be in the absence of the services trade restrictions, holding all other factors constant. The counterfactual comparison gives a behind-the-border 'tax equivalent,' if the restrictions have raised price-cost margins, or a behind-the-border 'productivity equivalent,' if the restrictions have raised real resource costs. Studies along these lines include the OECD studies of product market regulation (OECD 2005a, 2005b; Conway, Janod, and Nicoletti 2005; Findlay and Warren 2000; Kalirajan 2000; Kalirajan and others 2000; McGuire, Schuele, and Smith 2000; Nguyen-Hong 2000; Doove et al. 2001; Copenhagen Economics 2005; and OECD 2005c).

---

54. The first global project to capture restrictions in services was undertaken by the Productivity Commission of Australia. To date, this institution is one of the richest sources of databases on services restrictions. Unfortunately, many emerging countries such as Morocco and Tunisia were not included in the project. The OECD is another source of regulatory restrictiveness. However, in terms of coverage, only OECD countries are included. There are some differences between these two sources, especially in terms of weight given to different factors of restrictions. For detailed discussion of the OECD methodology, see Conway et al. (2005) and OECD (2005a, 2005b). For a discussion of the Australia Productivity Commission methodology, see Dee (2005) and McGuire, Schuele and Smith (2000).

license was granted to an operator specializing in the VSAT segment (leased lines), Divona.[55] The latest major development in the telecom market was the partial privatization of TT.[56] The 2001 law and the subsequent reforms enabled a dramatic change in the market structure of telecom services in Tunisia (Table 3.1).

Table 3.1. Players in the Fixed and Mobile Sectors and Ownership Structure

The Telecom Players		Ownership	Percentage Ownership	Market Share (%)
Fixed	Tunisie Telecom	Ministry of Communications	65%	100%
		Tecom (UAE)	35%	
Mobile	Tunisiana	Orascom Telecom (Egypt)	45%*	44%
		Wataniya (Kuwait)	50%*	
	Tunisie Telecom	Ministry of Communications	65%	56%
		Tecom (UAE)	35%	

*To our understanding, court case is in process to adjudicate percentage ownership.
Source: Global Insight, EMC 2006.

The reforms have also had a tremendous impact on the performance of the telecommunication sector, especially on the liberalized mobile segment. In four years, the number of mobile phones went from less than 400,000 to more than 6 million. By June 2006, the penetration rate reached 62 percent in 2006, one of the highest in the region (Rossotto and others 2007). Although the two ratios are not comparable, it is noticeable that the penetration of mobile phone surpassed that of fixed mobile as early as 2003, just two years after the opening of the sector (Figure 3.1). These developments reflect the tremendous increase in investments in telecom: the share of the latter in total gross capital formation increased from 2.6 percent in 1990 to 7.4 percent in 2005. As a result, the share of telecom in GDP tripled in 15 years, from 1.3 percent in 1990 to 4.3 percent in 2005.

The rapid increase in mobile phone penetration is not only the consequence of the new entrant's performance; the incumbent, TT, has also rapidly adapted to the more liberal environment and adjusted its strategy to meet the competition challenge. In 2006, TT enjoyed 56 percent of the mobile phone market, against 44 percent for the second operator Tunisiana (Figure 3.2).

Remaining Entry and Competition Barriers and Their Estimated Price Impacts. In spite of recent reforms, some restrictions to entry and competition remain. Under the GATS, in 1997, Tunisia undertook to bind, without limitation, measures affecting the supply of telex and packet-switched data transmission services as from 1999; mobile telephone, paging, teleconferencing and frame relay services as from 2000; and local telephone services as from January 2003.[57] However, it is stipulated that the supply of such services requires a start-up

---

55. Divona is a subsidiary of Monaco Telecom and Planete
56. 35 percent of its capital sold to a Dubai holding company, Tecom, for US$2.27 billion.
57. WTO document GATS/SC/87/Suppl.1, 11 April 1997.

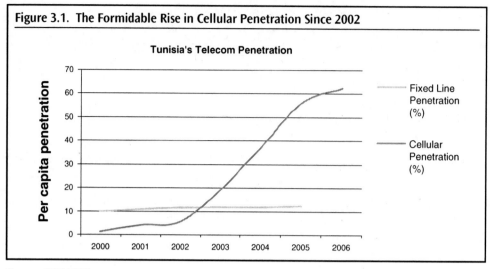

Figure 3.1. The Formidable Rise in Cellular Penetration Since 2002

Source: ITU 2006.

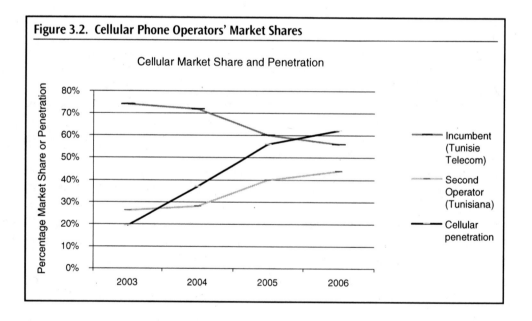

Figure 3.2. Cellular Phone Operators' Market Shares

and operating permit issued in the light of unspecified "national development needs." An operating permit is issued only with at least 51 percent of the equity held by Tunisians.

Tunisia has made no commitment concerning either long-distance or international telecommunications services or satellite services. Tunisia has not annexed the reference document on basic telecommunications to its Schedule of Commitments.[58] Nor do its commitments include the provisions of the WTO Annex on telecommunications services

---

58. The reference document specifies a number of measures for preventing large suppliers from adopting anti-competitive practices.

relating, *inter alia*, to leased circuits. During the negotiations in progress in the WTO in June 2005, Tunisia submitted a new offer on telecommunications services and indicated that the reference document will be annexed to their new Schedule of Commitments.

The current regulatory framework is characterized, in terms of entry and competition, by a few remaining barriers: (i) there are numerical restrictions on the number of carriers in both fixed and mobile telephony; (ii) in the fixed sector, local, domestic long distance and international long distance calls are still under the monopoly of TT (Table 3.2); (iii) In contrast with most emerging countries, courier services are highly restricted and private operators are required to operate in partnership with *Rapid Poste*; (iv) while the Internet market is open to the private sector, Tunisia's Internet Service Provider (ISPs) largely rely on the infrastructure of TT.[59] An exception to this is that high-usage subscribers can contract services from one of two VSAT ISPs. The lack of competition in infrastructure and the relatively high cost of VSAT subscription limit the benefits to consumers and finally, (v) the regulation of the sector is still fragmented and the INT is yet to become fully independent.

The monopoly in fixed line telephony is one factor holding back internet penetration. To illustrate, although Tunisia has more computers per head of population than Morocco—5.6 per 100 inhabitants in 2005, compared with 2.3 per 100 inhabitants in Morocco—its internet penetration is lower—9.4 users per 100 inhabitants in 2005, compared with 14.6 users per 100 inhabitants in Morocco (ITU 2006). One can also relate the restriction in access to the fixed infrastructure to the fact that Tunisia trails behind international benchmarks in secure internet servers, bandwidth, Internet hosts and broadband subscribers (see Rossotto and others 2007).[60]

Table 3.2. Competitive Structure by Segment of the Telecom Market

Fixed	Local	Domestic Long Distance	Int'l Long Distance
State of Competition	Monopoly	Monopoly	Monopoly
Leading Players	Tunisie Telecom	Tunisie Telecom	Tunisie Telecom
Mobile	2G	2.5G	3G
State of Competition	Competition	Competition	Yet to be licensed
Leading Players	Tunisie Telecom, Tunisiana	Tunisie Telecom, Tunisiana	—

Source: Global Insight

59. Internet traffic passes through lines leased to TT (via the *Agence tunisienne de l'Internet* (ATI—Tunisian Internet Agency—a public corporation) at prices and under access conditions determined by the latter.

60. The burden of investment for upgrading the network in the areas of broadband and bandwidth for the corporate, outsourcing and tourism markets fall largely on Tunisie Telecom (i.e., the government). TT has made significant investments in recent years: The incumbent is adding ADSL lines and a new broadband network, which the government intends to use as the platform for universal access to broadband Internet facilities by 2009, and it is investing in a 102-km runner cable to link the operator's international facilities with the new SEA ME WE 4 submarine cable (when complete, the SEA ME WE 4 network will run 20,000 km between France and Singapore, via Algeria, Tunisia, Italy, Egypt, Saudi Arabia, the United Arab Emirates, Pakistan, India, Sri Lanka, Bangladesh, Thailand and Malaysia). All these reforms will increase bandwidth; however the segment's leadership remains with one firm, and would almost certainly be carried out more effectively in a competitive market, for example from the quality and fiscal perspectives.

Cross-country analysis of restrictions in telecom shows that a large number of countries discriminates against foreign providers (national treatment limitations) (Figure 3.3). The restrictions (market access and national treatment limitations) in Tunisia are not as severe as those in Vietnam and Thailand but they are worse than those in Malaysia, Bulgaria, and Romania, and significantly higher than those in Morocco. Tunisia's general restrictions on competition could currently be inflating the prices of domestically owned telecommunications services by about 7 percent, while the additional restrictions on foreign ownership mean that the prices from foreign suppliers could be inflated by about 15 percent (see Figure 3.3 and annex in Rossotto and others 2007).[61] Among emerging countries, Morocco, Chile and Estonia have the most open telecom sector. These countries apply no discrimination between players.

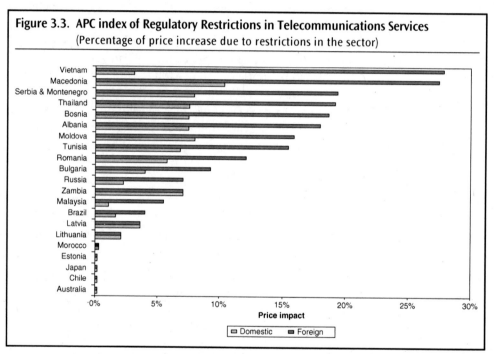

Figure 3.3. APC index of Regulatory Restrictions in Telecommunications Services
(Percentage of price increase due to restrictions in the sector)

Source: Based on OECD (2005b). Data for Morocco collected in Tunisia by Bank staff.

Reform Options. Although the removal of the legal monopoly of TT in the area of mobile telephony and Internet service provision is a positive move, further reforms remain essential. The remarkable progress achieved in mobile telephony confirms the need for pursuing the liberalization process. Tunisia could thus (i) lift the numerical restrictions on the number of carriers in both fixed and mobile telephony, to increase the general contestability of the market and (ii) lift the foreign ownership limits on competitive carriers,

---

61. This effect has been quantified in second-stage econometric work by Warren (2000), as summarized in Dee (2005a).

to attract further foreign direct investment.[62] These two reforms would have two types of effects. First, the greater market contestability and foreign competition would squeeze price-cost margins within telecommunications. Were Tunisia to remove these restrictions, price-cost margins would be squeezed, and prices would be lower accordingly. The reform could thus generate non-negligible price reductions.

A second possible effect of telecommunications reform is a productivity improvement in wholesale and retail trade, as a result of greater use of the internet for B2B ecommerce (Box 3.2)

Box 3.2. Potential Rippling Effects of Liberalizing Telecom on Wholesale-Retail Margins

A Japanese study reported in Hertel, Walmsley and Itakura (2001) finds that the use of ecommerce for B2B transactions could reduce wholesale-retail margins from 19.6 percent to 4.9 percent of prices—a 75 percent reduction in wholesale-retail margins themselves, equivalent to a 300 percent productivity improvement in wholesale and retail trade—when B2B commerce is in use. Even in Japan, internet penetration is by no means universal, so the sector-wide cost savings are diluted accordingly.

The Hertel, Walmsley, and Itakura (2001) study suggests an average 2 percent penetration rate across Japanese agriculture, manufacturing and services, with up to 14 percent penetration in autos, while ITU statistics give 50.2 internet users per 100 inhabitants in Japan. If Tunisia were to increase its internet penetration rate to that of Morocco, and to achieve cost savings comparable to that in Japan, it would be equivalent to a 0.6 percent improvement in productivity across the entire wholesale and retail trade sector, with benefits spread throughout the economy, including in services and manufacturing.

The Financial Sector

The financial sector plays a central role in the process of capital accumulation and productivity growth. As a large industry in itself, it contributes directly to growth. They account for about 5 percent of GDP in Tunisia. But the indirect contribution of the financial sector to growth is even more important as efficient financial intermediaries promote investment and growth by facilitating trade, mobilizing and allocating savings, and helping manage risks. Further financial deepening is thus essential for lowering the cost of financing and promoting productive investment.

Recent Reforms. Tunisia has undertaken major reforms to improve the legal and regulatory framework of the financial sector, privatize state banks, and enhance competition in the financial sector. On the *legal and regulatory front,* recent reforms have focused on reducing non-performing loans (which stand around 20 percent in 2006), improving bank governance, increasing transparency and accountability and strengthening the regulatory framework (FSAP + IMF paper).[63] Following the promulgation of a new law for the *Banque*

---

62. If the option is to keep a very gradual approach, then rapidly allowing the entry of another operator in the fixed telephony can help boost investments in that segment and further reduce prices.

63. High level of Non Performing Loans (NPL) is the legacy of past directed credit policies and provision of credit to unprofitable public enterprises.

Centrale de Tunisie (BCT) in May 2006, measures are taken to strengthen banks' credit policies and banks are required to increase provisioning for NPLs. In this connection, the tax deductibility of provisions for NPLs was increased and legal reforms were introduced to accelerate the sale of collateral. The new law gives the BCT new authority in the area of advisory assistance, monitoring, transparency, supervision, and publication of economic and financial information. As for monetary policy, this new law emphasizes that price stability is the main objective of the central bank with the policy interest rate as the main instrument.

As part of the *pro-competitive agenda of reform* (privatization and market opening), two public banks have been privatized and a number of private banks were recapitalized. Tunisia sold one large state bank to a major private French bank (Societe Generale) in early 2002, and another one to a Moroccan-Spanish banking consortium in 2005. The autonomously measures taken to enhance competition in the sector include: (i) the removal of many restrictions on supply of financial services under Mode 3 (commercial presence). For instance the foreign equity majority ownership limitations have been lifted. Foreign investors can now become majority shareholders of a bank in Tunisia. Furthermore there is no more need for foreign banks to set-up a joint venture to enter the Tunisian market; (ii) the lifting of restrictions on temporary intra-corporate movements (Mode 4). Although the managing director of an institution must be a Tunisian national, foreigners can be board members; (iii) the simplification of entry requirements. The opening of bank branches is now conditional to a simple specification by the BCT of terms and conditions rather than a license; the opening of a bank, subject to the acquisition of a license, should be theoretically faster now, as decision about the application should be notified to the concerned parties within a period of four months after submission.

Although the approach to reforming the financial sector is mostly unilateral, Tunisia has made specific commitments in the financial services sector under the GATS.[64] These commitments were improved by an offer which became definitive on February 26, 1998.[65] This new schedule, attached to the Fifth Protocol annexed to the GATS, replaced the section relating to financial services in the April 1994 offer, the insurance commitments remaining unchanged. The revised version of Tunisia's Schedule of Commitments under the GATS binds, without limitation, the measures affecting the cross-border supply or consumption abroad of several financial services, including those provided by banks, leasing companies and investment companies.[66] In reality, the foreign exchange controls sharply restrict the opportunities for cross-border trade, apart from the financing of current operations.[67] In fact, most financial operations, such as investments in foreign stocks and bonds, are not authorized, inasmuch as residents (whether natural or legal persons) cannot freely send foreign currency abroad or receive it from abroad, no more than they can purchase financial services abroad. Measures affecting the supply (by any mode, except Mode 4) of loan broking and financial consultancy services are bound without limitation.

Market Structure and Performance. Thanks to continuous reforms, Tunisia has the second most developed financial system in the region (after Morocco), with total assets

---

64. WTO document GATS/SC/87, 15 April 1994.
65. WTO document GATS/SC/87/Suppl.2, 26 February 1998.
66. Public limited companies for the promotion of investment—fixed capital (SICAF) or risk capital (SICAR).
67. Stephenson, S. (1999).

Table 3.3. Tunisia Financial Sector Structure between 2000 and 2004

Type of Institution	2000			2006		
	Institutions	Total Assets (in MD)	% GDP	Institutions	Total Assets (in MD)	% GDP
Commercial banks	15	35,412.2	86.7	13	19613	73.5
state controlled	5	15,601.8	38.2	5	11676	43.8
Private	10	19,810.4	48.5	8	7936	29.7
Ex-development banks	5	1,334.1	3.3	6	1119	4.2
Off-shore banks	8	2,777.9	6.8	8	1961	7.3
Postal savings	1	1,630.0	4.0	1	800	3
Postal checking system	1	1,653.0	4.0	1	1000	3.7
Leasing companies	11	1,295.7	3.2	9	861	3.2
Factoring companies	2	108.9	0.3	2	30	0.1
Total	58	79,624	195.0	53	44,996	168.5

Source: BCT.

equivalent to about 90 percent of GDP. The system is dominated by banks, with the domestic bond and equity markets playing a very limited role in savings mobilization. The banking system in a broad sense (comprising all establishments under the control of the Central Bank of Tunisia) includes 20 commercial banks (of which five are development banks recently converted into full-service banks, one microfinance bank, and one SME financing bank), 8 offshore banks, 9 leasing companies, 2 factoring companies, and 2 merchant banks (Table 3.3). The non-bank financial sector comprises a large and growing number of (mostly bank-owned) mutual funds (34 in 2006) and venture capital companies (38 in 2006);[68] 2 pension funds and 16 insurance companies. Following the 2002 and 2005 privatizations, the market share of public banks declined from to 37.2 to 30.6 percent in 2006. At present, the state banks, the local private banks, and the foreign banks now have roughly equal market shares. The four leading banks (in terms of assets) account for about 56 percent of total commercial bank assets and the five foreign clearing banks operating in Tunisia represent 20 percent of total bank assets. The current policy priority is to merge and privatize five small state banks recently converted to commercial banks and owned jointly with the governments of certain GCC countries as well as Libya.

The Tunis Stock Exchange is small. The insurance sector is supervised by a Directorate General of the Ministry of Finance, and the securities markets by an autonomous *Conseil du Marché Financier* reporting directly to the President of the Republic. Control over state-owned financial institutions is exercised through the Ministry of Finance.

---

68. SICARs (Sociétés d'Investissement a capital-risque) have grown in number from 26 to 38 between 2000 and 2004. However they still play a limited role in the financial sector with hardly 1.2 percent of the financial sector's assets.

Increased competition in the sector has had some short-term costs—notably in terms of lower profitability for less efficient domestic banks—but overall has benefited the economy as a whole as evidenced by the increase in credits allocated to the private sector at a lower cost. Indeed, the return on asset (ROA) and the return on equity (ROE) have sharply decreased between 2000 and 2005 amounting respectively 0.61 percent and 7.05 against 1.6 and 12.5 percent between 1995 and 2000 (Dia 2007). The pattern of interest margins also points to a decline in profitability driven by competition. Interest rate margins among Tunisian banks declined from 4.6 percent in 2000 to 3.1 percent in 2004. It is noteworthy that interest margin levels in Tunisia are slightly lower than in neighboring Morocco (3.7) but still above the 2.0 percent average in the EU. This suggests that more competition is occurring within the EU banking sector. In any case, the winners of the increased competition are Tunisian consumers. Figure 3.4 suggests that consumers rather than firms have benefited proportionally more from increased competition. The share of consumer credit in total credit to the private sector increased from 16 percent in 2000 to 20 percent in 2005.

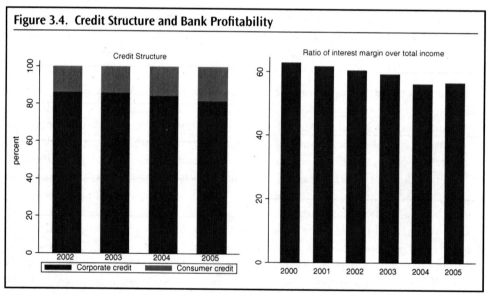

Figure 3.4. Credit Structure and Bank Profitability

Source: BCT.

Remaining Barriers to Competition and Their Estimated Price Impacts. To further enhance the competitiveness of the banking sector further reforms are needed as many restrictions to competition remain. Indeed (i) the foreign exchange controls sharply restrict the opportunities for cross-border trade, apart from the financing of current operations. Foreign-based banks cannot lend funds on the local market and resident banks are not allowed to offer credits abroad or invest in foreign stocks and bonds. However non-resident companies are free to acquire financial services abroad in foreign currency; (ii) under mode 3, any takeover exceeding 50 percent of the capital of a bank is subjected to an authorization of the CSI; (iii) regarding the type of services banks can provide restrictions still exit. Banks cannot directly offer other services (such as insurance products) than banking services.[69]

Cross-country analysis using the PCA index shows that Tunisia's banking restrictions against foreign banks are not as severe as those in Malaysia, China, Vietnam and Brazil. Yet, they are marginally worse than those in Morocco, and significantly worse than those in South Eastern Europe. Tunisia's score reflects mainly the restrictions on both lending and raising funds that are faced by foreign banks and the constraints imposed by foreign exchange controls on domestic banks.

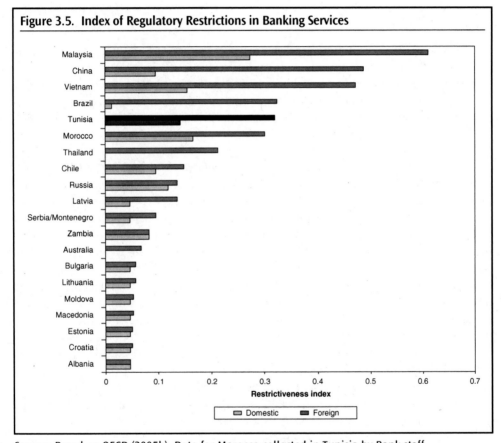

Figure 3.5. Index of Regulatory Restrictions in Banking Services

Source: Based on OECD (2005b). Data for Morocco collected in Tunisia by Bank staff.

Reform Options. A higher degree of competition and efficiency in the banking system would contribute to greater financial stability, product innovation, and access by households and firms to financial services, which in turn can improve the prospects for economic

---

69. It is also noteworthy that off-shore banks dedicated to serve non-resident companies operate under less restrictive regulation on this regard. They are authorized to engage in all banking operations with non-residents. With respect to residents companies, off-shore banks may also offer financing to them but only using their foreign exchange or foreign currency borrowings resources.

growth. Achieving a higher degree of competition and efficiency in the Tunisian financial sector will require (i) further encouraging and facilitating entry into the banking sector to further stimulate competition while continuing to strengthen risk management practices; (ii) lifting the restrictions faced by foreign banks in lending and raising funds domestically; and (iii) strengthening the regulatory oversight by finding ways to enforce the legal texts.

According to our estimates, the increment in the cost of banking services due to the removal of market access and national treatment restrictions (above measures) could decline from 7.5 percent to about 5 percent for domestic banks and from 17.5 per cent to 7 percent for foreign banks (Appendix E).

Professional Services

Professional services (accounting, legal and engineering services) are another set of important services that intermediate transactions and affect firms' efficiency. As a result, efficiently delivered professional services, and lower prices, benefit the whole economy. For Tunisia, the availability of a large pool of well-trained professionals also makes the sector an important potential source of export earnings and export diversification (see chapter for details regarding the sector's market structure, performance and prospects).

Entry and Competition Barriers and Their Estimated Price Impacts. Until recently, professional services were mainly perceived as having to be protected from foreign competition rather than as dynamic activities with a strong export potential. As shown in chapter 4, today, Tunisia's professional services sectors face two major restrictions: (i) strict requirement that partners of firms in these sectors should be local (restrictions on commercial presence and FDI) and; (ii) strict nationality requirement to enter the law and accounting sectors.[70] These restrictions were put in place in a different world, where professional services were not conceived as a tradable good. Today, with the possibilities offered by technological development, Tunisia has a strong interest in allowing more private and foreign investments in the sector, in order to boost exports. As shown in the ICT sector, there are strong synergies possible between Mode 3 imports and Mode 1 exports.

Cross-country analysis using OECD restrictiveness indices show that Tunisia has a relatively liberal regime in the engineering sector but scores relatively poorly in legal and accounting services. In engineering, Tunisia has been trying to encourage FDI, and accordingly provides a relatively unrestrictive regulatory regime for both the domestic and foreign engineers required for large projects. On the other hand, Tunisia's range of regulations, particularly on fees, make it second only to Turkey and Italy in restricting competition in accounting, and second only to Greece and Turkey in restricting competition in law. What the OECD index fails to indicate is the strength of Tunisia's discriminatory restrictions in these professions—foreign firms cannot practice law, but can only provide legal consulting services, and accounting firms must be 100 percent locally owned.[71]

---

70. There are a few foreign lawyers and law offices registered in Tunisia as providers of *legal consultancy services* only, subject to the provisions of the Investment Incentives Code. These lawyers are supervised at national level by the *Ordre des avocats tunisiens* (Tunisian Bar Association).

71. OECD questionnaires for professional services are largely restricted to measures that are non-discriminatory—for example, exclusive licensing, and restrictions on fees, advertising and the legal form of business.

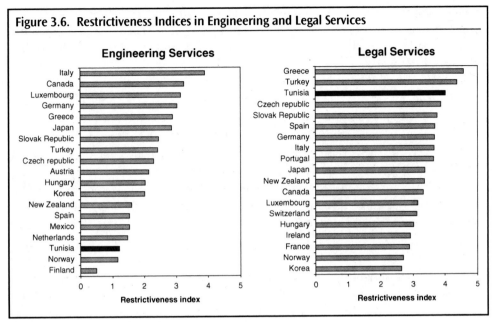

Figure 3.6. Restrictiveness Indices in Engineering and Legal Services

Source: Based on OECD (2005a).

Reform Options. The lack of competition resulting from the above restrictions typically inflates transaction costs in the economy. So, lifting them could help reduce prices of professional services at least to some extent, because several other factors play a role in determining the price of professional services. According to our estimations, removing nationality requirement and allowing locally licensed foreign partners in Tunisia's professional services market would reduce the price impact of services trade restrictions from an estimated 19 percent to 12 percent for foreign services suppliers (Appendix Table E.1). Additional bilateral concessions in the context of the Tunisia-EU Association Agreement (AA) could further reduce the price impact of remaining restrictions on the supply of foreign professional services in Tunisia to about 6 percent (bottom of Appendix Table E.1), with a corresponding improvement in the competitiveness of Tunisian suppliers into the EU market.[72]

Reducing these restrictions, however, should be envisaged as an integral part of Tunisia's strategy to effectively participate in global production networks. First, Tunisia is a country rich in well-qualified and internationally competitive human resources in certain professional services, such as accounting and engineering. Second, there is a strong link between services exports and commercial presence (or FDI imports). For instance, in Tunisia's ICT sector where FDI are unrestricted, many foreign companies have entered the market of business process outsourcing (BPO) and set up branches in order to export services back to the parent or third-country client. The same phenomenon can be anticipated if commercial presence is allowed in accounting, law and engineering sectors.

Further, since trade in professional services is also largely based on the movement of natural persons, Tunisian providers of professional services are particularly affected by

---

72. Out-of-sample extrapolation on Tunisia based on econometric work by Nguyen-Hong 2000.

regulations which restrict such movement: visa restrictions, not automatic recognition of qualifications, and so forth. Tunisia would benefit from enhanced market access conditions to the EU market. International cooperation, especially with EU countries, is thus crucial to secure greater market access.

In sum, given the nature of the restrictions in the professional services sectors in Tunisia and in its major export markets, pro-competitive reform agenda in the professional services sector could have the following two elements. First, Tunisia could unilaterally relax the requirement in law and accounting for partners to be local, with partners only required to be locally licensed. The corresponding nationality requirement affecting the entry in the accounting and engineering services markets could be removed to allow greater competition and reduce transaction costs. Second, Tunisia could seek bilateral concessions in the context of its Association Agreement with the EU, in order to facilitate the outsourcing of back-office accounting and legal services to Tunisia, especially from France. This may entail two elements:

- ◾ A mutual recognition agreement with France and other EU countries could be sought, allowing recognition of local Tunisian professional qualifications for the purposes of undertaking the back office activities; In France, under Mode 4, non-EU intra-corporate transferees, business visitors, and contractual service suppliers may be permitted to provide services, by a decision of the Ministry of Finance in agreement with the Ministry of Foreign Affairs, with a residence requirement not to exceed five years. However, national treatment and market access for independent providers remain unbound except as provided in the horizontal section. If Tunisia is interested in securing market access for independent provider, negotiation with France will be needed.
- ◾ Arrangements for a systematic granting of visas to specific professions for the purpose of temporary provision of services to EU countries can also be sought. The involvement of professional services associations and their commitment to abide by any agreement reached will be crucial.

The Air Transport Sector

The aviation sector is regarded by the authorities as one of the strategic sectors for the development of the Tunisian economy; it generates substantial hard currency income, accounts for 2 per cent of GDP and provides about 12,000 jobs. The competitiveness and development of tourism is in particular strongly dependent on the efficiency and cost of air transport.

Recent Reforms and Current Market Structure. The Government's current strategy is to encourage private participation in civil aviation activities in order to improve the profitability of domestic air transport and air freight services, in view of the important role played by these two activities in the development of the national economy. Another Government objective is to continue "upgrading" the public corporations TUNISAIR, TUNINTER and NOUVELAIR. A new private air transport company KARTHAGO began operating in March 2002.

The Civil Aviation Code, the main legislation on air transport, was amended in 2004.[73] Once the implementing decrees are in place, the Code will enable a broad range of services to be opened up to the private sector. One of the draft decrees lays down the conditions which an enterprise must fulfill in order to build, equip, operate, maintain and develop airports. Another is intended to harmonize the Tunisian regulations with European standards concerning the technical and financial conditions for obtaining a permit to operate an airline.

Entry and Competition Barriers and Their Estimated Price Impacts. Since 1996, non-scheduled (charter) air freight and passenger transport activities have been open to private initiative, provided that a majority of the enterprise's equity is held by Tunisian nationals.[74] Scheduled international passenger transport services are provided by the state-owned, TunisAir, by one of the other Tunisian companies, or by foreign enterprises under bilateral traffic-sharing agreements. Cabotage is reserved for Tunisian enterprises. On the domestic market, passenger and freight tariffs are regulated.[75] Passenger fares, freight tariffs and the terms of transport between Tunisia and other countries are subject to the provisions of air transport agreements.

The Government supports the principle of progressive liberalization of air transport within the framework of a regional free trade market or in the international context. TunisAir has recently signed strategic alliance agreements with Air France and Royal Air Maroc. The bilateral agreements with the member countries of the European Union are scheduled to be amended to permit multiple designations (see below). Tunisia has no open sky agreement with any country but has been offered to participate to EU common sky along with other MEDA countries.

Cross-country analysis of openness in air transport reveals that Tunisia's restrictions in air passenger transport are second only to Hungary, because Tunisia has not entered into an open skies agreement with the United States or regionally, because the rates are regulated for domestic aviation, and because the government still retains majority ownership in the largest carrier (Figure 3.7).

To quantify the price impact of restrictions, the econometric work by Gonenc and Nicoletti (2000) and Doove et al. (2001) has been updated using more recent information about the content of air services agreements from ICAO (2004). The price impact of Tunisia's current air services agreements with the EU has been quantified at 15.4 per cent. This would drop to zero in a bilateral basis under an open skies agreement (Table 3.4). This price reduction is likely to come about through a reduction in price-costs margins rather than through a reduction in resource costs. Cost savings from achieving greater network economies would probably require a more extensive series of open skies agreements.

Reform Options. It is not sensible to attempt to liberalize air transport unilaterally. Indeed, if Tunisia were to liberalize, while its partners continued to restrict entry, capacity and airfares, this could lead to adverse outcomes for Tunisia's aviation industry, without

---

73. Law No. 99-58 of 29 June 1999, as amended and supplemented by Law No. 2004-57 of 12 July 2004.

74. Order of 04/05/1996 publishing the specifications establishing the conditions for granting authorization to operate air freight transport services; and Order of 28 February 1995 specifying the conditions for granting authorization to operate non-scheduled air passenger transport services.

75. Decree No. 95-1142 of 28 June 1995.

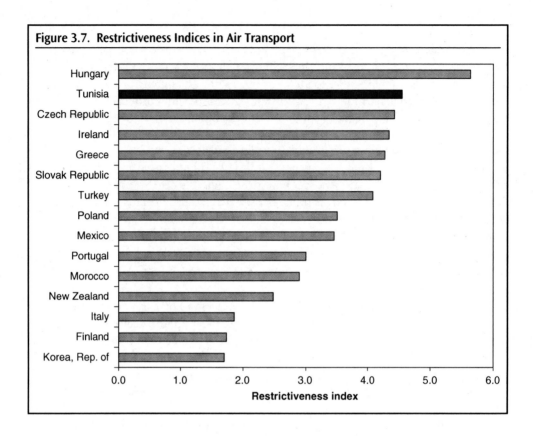

Figure 3.7. Restrictiveness Indices in Air Transport

Table 3.4. Direct Price Impacts of Bilateral Air Service Agreements

Destination Countries	Origin Countries			
	Tunisia	EU	GAFTA	Rest of World
Currently				
Tunisia	na	15.4	15.9	14.2
EU	15.4	0	12.3	16.9
GAFTA	15.5	12.3	15.9	14.9
Rest of world	14.2	18.2	14.9	18.3
After Tunisian open skies agreement with EU				
Tunisia	na	0	15.9	14.2
EU	0	0	12.3	16.9
GAFTA	15.5	12.3	15.9	14.9
Rest of world	14.2	18.2	14.9	18.3

Source: Updated from Dee (2005a), and based on Doove and others (2001).

providing benefits to its consumers. The most sensible first step to further liberalization of air transport in Tunisia would be a *bilateral* "open skies" agreement with the European Union, Tunisia's major economic partner. This would open EU-Tunisia bilateral routes up to low-cost carriers, putting competitive pressure on airfares on those routes. In the medium term, an open skies agreements with Tunisia's Arab League partners would provide the maximum opportunity for Tunisia to optimize its own international air services network, and hence achieve the full cost savings available from reaping network economies.

At present, like the other ENP countries, Tunisia faces two issues in its aviation policy vis-à-vis the EU. First, it will have to negotiate "horizontal" agreements replacing nationality restrictions in designation articles with a non-discrimination Community designation clause. In practical terms, it means that one agreement with the EU will replaced bilateral agreements with the EU-member states. Needless to add that the shift in the EU of aviation policy responsibilities from the national level to that of the European Commission (EC) level significantly weakens negotiating position of all other countries including ENP partners, and therefore Tunisia. The EC will certainly be more sensitive to the "average" interest of the EU than to specific national interests that reflect privileged relationships that a particular member might have vis-à-vis Tunisia.

Second, the Tunisian government will have to decide whether to accept or reject the EU's offer of an "open skies" arrangement. The EU external aviation road-map, adopted by the European Council in 2005, envisages participation of the ENP countries in *Internal Aviation market* scheduled to enter into force by 2010. Participation to the *Internal market* does not amount to the extensions of various provisions of bilateral agreements to new "horizontal" agreements but it would effectively remove all restraints present in bilateral agreements. It sets a country on the path of regulatory convergence of its external aviation framework toward that of the *acquis communautaire.*

Morocco's "open skies" agreement signed in 2006 with the EU is the first signed by a partner outside of Europe illustrates the challenges and opportunities offered by the EU offer. The Morocco agreement lays out two phases to Morocco's participation in the EU Single Aviation Market. During the first phase, Morocco will integrate the EU aviation rules—aviation safety, air traffic management, environment, consumer protection, computer reservation systems—into the regulatory regime of its aviation sector.[76] Market access restrictions will also be partially released during this phase. Upon ratification of the open skies agreement by the EU and Morocco's compliance with EU regulatory aviation safety standards, Moroccan air carriers will be able, in a second phase, to fly to and through any airport in Europe provided that they depart from Morocco. EU airlines departing from Europe will be entitled to operate without restriction between any point in Europe and any point in Morocco.

An "open skies" agreement with the EU is thus a bold way of adopting aviation policies and institutions that have proved to be extremely effective in boosting the development of the aviation sector in highly developed countries. Deeper integration through regulatory convergence with a highly developed partner creates new economic and investment opportunities thanks to the establishment of a satisfactory level playing field with fair and equitable

---

76. This first phase is scheduled to last 24 months. It will begin once the Agreement is ratified by all parties (25 states and Morocco) and safety arrangements are deemed satisfactory.

competition conditions. While the regulatory and legal requirements for participation to EU acquis is challenging (see Appendix B), Tunisia will not start from scratch in some areas (a number of measures bringing security and safety norms up to the international/EU standards have already been implemented). In other cases, EU rules only apply beyond certain thresholds that Tunisia, because of its level of air aviation activity, will not cross in the short-to-medium term. Such examples include airport noise (kicks in only above a certain number of departures), competition in ground-handling (applies only above a certain number of passengers/cargo) and rules on slot allocation (in the case of capacity limitations).

On pure economic terms, accepting an "open skies" agreement with the EU would yield welfare gains for Tunisia. The issue is how to minimize adjustment cost and convince those who resist the reform. In that respect, the lessons from the Moroccan experience are instructive (see Box 3.3).

Box 3.3. Making Reform a Reality: The Moroccan Experience

On purely economic welfare maximization grounds, the question is not whether Tunisia an opens skies agreement with the EU will be positive but rather how to go about it. The latter boils down to two questions: How to overcome inevitable resistance from Tunis Air? How to sequence reform measures in order to avoid excessive adjustment costs?

The Morocco's experience offers insights to answers to both of these questions. In more general terms, it shows that benefits from regional integration into a more developed partner do not come by default but call for an activist government approach to exploiting them and aviation reform should be part of a broader reform package removing binding constraints in complementary areas. In more specific terms, for political economy reasons, aviation reforms should be directly linked to a broader strategy of development of tourism and the decisions should be made how a national air carrier would fit this strategy. Moroccan government used the RAM as a tool of its tourism development program while simultaneously prompting its restructuring in provision of its core functions. Without a detailed assessment of strengths and weaknesses of Tunis Air, it would be impossible to tell whether this model would be viable in Tunisia. Whatever the answer might be, the bottom line is that the key to boosting trade in service is creating a competitive framework for the aviation sector instead of protecting national carrier.

As far as the sequencing issue is concerned, the government should begin removing constraints on landing rights for EU-based carriers, bringing safety measures and management of airports in line with the EU acquis communautaire. Another important lesson worth emulating is an active search for EU-based LCCs to launch their operations in Tunisia. These steps, which are "win-win" propositions, should be taken even before the open skies negotiations begin.

How Would Reforms Affect the Economy?

The Reform Scenarios

This chapter conducted two sets of simulations to determine the economy-wide effects of further liberalizing the telecommunications, banking, air transport and professional services: the first looked at partial reform and the second at full reform.

■ The partial reform options are those discussed in the sector-by-sector analysis of the previous section—these reforms represent feasible targets, but address just a subset of the universe of discriminatory and non-discriminatory restrictions out there. The first set of simulations thus consists of unilaterally removing some of the restrictions in banking and telecommunication sectors, and reciprocally liberalizing the professions and air transport with the EU.[77]

▪ Full reform is a theoretical scenario that would remove *all* the restrictions to entry and business conduct identified in the benchmarking exercise and that would take into account interaction effects between sectoral reforms. More specifically, all the discriminatory and non-discriminatory restrictions in banking, telecom, and the professions are eliminated entirely, while air transport is liberalized on a bilateral basis with the EU.

The effects of the suggested reform initiatives have been projected using the FTAP model developed by Dee and Hanslow (2001). This model differs from the GTAP model (from which it is derived) by treating foreign direct investment, an important mode by which services are delivered. It also differs from single-country models (such as Van Der Mensbrugghe 2005) by including a full representation of other regions, including their tariffs and barriers to services trade, so that it can fully capture bilateral and multilateral liberalization scenarios, not just unilateral ones (see Box 3.4).

The Results: Welfare Gains from Services Liberalization

The effects of the above Tunisian services trade liberalization scenarios on economic well-being in each region are shown in Table E.3. The effects of partial reforms are not very large in absolute terms but quite large in relation of the sectoral value-added in some of the sectors. The economy is also projected to be slightly larger, with real GDP being 0.3 percent larger than otherwise.

The reason the gains are small is that most current restrictions to entry and business in banking, telecom and air transport inflate price-cost margins, rather than increase real resource costs. In other words, the prices of services have been inflated, not because the real resource cost of producing them has been inflated, but because incumbent firms have been able to earn economic rents—akin to a tax, but with the revenue flowing to the incumbents rather than to government. Liberalization of these barriers yields in producer and consumer surplus associated with improvements in allocative efficiency, but also has redistributive effects associated with the elimination of rents to incumbents. The net result is a large transfer from incumbent producers to consumers and other using industries, and a relatively small gain to the economy as a whole. Although the net welfare gain is small, Tunisian consumers would secure a large gain with liberalization of telecom, banking, and air transport.

This is in contrast to the situation of services trade restrictions in the profession, which partially increase the real resource cost of doing business. Liberalization is then equivalent to a productivity improvement (saving in real resources), and yields gains associated with a greater efficiency of firms (downward shift in supply curves). This can increase returns for the incumbent service providers, as well as lowering costs for users elsewhere in the economy. The net result is a relatively large gain to the economy as a whole.

---

77. The telecommunication sector is not included in the simulations because Morocco has gone much of the way in liberalizing it, and the welfare impact of further liberalization would be small.

Box 3.4. Methodological Approach: The FTAP Model

The FTAP model is a computable general equilibrium model incorporating services delivered via FDI. It differs in turn from GTAP (Hertel 1997), the 'plain vanilla' model from which it was derived, in three important respects. First, because many services are delivered primarily via commercial presence, the modeling framework includes foreign direct investment as a mode of services trade delivery, and covers separately the production and trading activity of foreign multinationals. In other words, GTAP, the conventional multi-country model, is split out by ownership as well as location. In the current version of FTAP, the foreign owner-ship shares for Morocco were obtained from WTO (2003). The relative sizes of the Moroccan communications, insurance and other financial services industries were adjusted upwards, and other transport services adjusted downwards, compared with those in the original GTAP database, based on value added shares from the latest Moroccan input-output table for 2003.

Second, by virtue of foreign ownership, at least some of the profits of foreign multinationals will be repatriated back to the home countries. Thus the profit streams in the conventional multi-country model have to be reallocated from the host to the home country, after provision is made for them to be taxed in either the home or host country. This reallocation leads to a distinction between GDP—the income generated in a region—and GNP—the income received by residents of a region. The latter forms the basis of (although is not identical to) the welfare measure in FTAP. The information on profit repatriation comes from the Balance of Payments Statistics of the IMF.

Finally, not all profits of foreign multinationals need be repatriated to the home country. Some may be reinvested in the host country. To account for this phenomenon, and to allow for the effect that regulatory reform may have on both domestic and foreign direct invest-ment more generally, the model makes provision for savings and capital accumulation. This is particularly important, because some regulatory barriers are aimed directly at limiting foreign equity participation. It is therefore important to capture how regulatory reform will affect not just foreign ownership shares, but also the total amount of productivity capacity available to an economy. National savings rates are derived from the macroeco-nomic data in the International Financial Statistics and Balance of Payments Statistics of the IMF. Government savings rates are derived from the Government Finance Statistics of the IMF. Household savings rates are calculated as a residual. The FTAP model also dif-fers from GTAP in other respects. In particular, it allows for firm-level product differenti-ation. This is also important, since services tend to be highly specialized, being tailored to the needs of individual customers. The corresponding Dixit-Stiglitz preferences mean that the model picks up endogenous productivity gains from greater variety of products or ser-vices. This is in addition to the exogenous productivity gains from reform of cost-raising regulatory barriers in services.

The model contains four regions—Tunisia, the EU, the GAFTA, and the rest of the world—It contains 30 sectors, including 11 in the services sector (Appendix table E.2).[78] An inno-vative feature of the model is the distinction of firms' capital according to its origin, which allows simulating the impact of the rights of establishment (mode 3 transactions). The for-eign ownership share of capital in Tunisia's sectors in the model, based on information from the WTO (WTO 2003) is as follows: communications 36 percent, banking and insurance 31 percent, maritime transport 3 percent, air transport 3 percent and professional services 17 percent.

---

78. Note that tourism is included in the model as a sales activity rather than a separate productive industry. This means that sales to foreign tourists are recorded among the exports of the industries pro-ducing goods that foreign tourists buy (air passenger transport, and so on), while sales to domestic tourists are recorded among the sales to household consumption of those industries.

The above reform scenarios were concentrated in sectors where barriers appear to create rents. In addition, the reform measures were largely aimed at removing discrimination against foreign suppliers. This is no coincidence. When regulatory restrictions are targeted only at foreign suppliers, they tend to be explicit quantity controls, since this is the most feasible way of imposing discrimination.

The gains modeled here are significantly smaller than those in the Konan and Maskus (2004) study of the impact of services liberalization in Tunisia. As noted, those authors simply assumed that barriers to foreign direct investment were half rent-creating and half cost-escalating. On the basis of this assumption, their projected gains in economic well-being from services trade liberalization were about 4 percent. By contrast, when they assumed the barriers to be entirely rent-creating, their projected gains in economic well-being fell to 0.33 percent, close to that projected here. In the current study, the treatment of barriers is based on available empirical evidence, where available, rather than assumption.

Another reason for the gains in the Konan and Maskus (2004) to be slightly bigger is that they implicitly assumed that the services of domestic and foreign-owned firms in Tunisia were perfect substitutes (they did not explicitly identify the proportion of each industry that was foreign-owned, but assumed that the reduction in barriers to foreign investment would affect the prices of all firms in Tunisia, not just the foreign-owned firms). By contrast, the GTAP model assumes that the services of domestic and foreign-owned firms are close but imperfect substitutes. This also reduces the gains from reform slightly, but this is of second order importance, compared to the different treatment of the barriers themselves (as the Konan and Maskus sensitivity analysis shows).

Finally, gains in reforming services sectors depend on the number and nature of services reformed. The point is demonstrated by studies that have looked at the impact of more widespread reforms in services, including reform of the non-discriminatory restrictions in wholesale and retail trade, electricity generation and ports, where costs have been raised. These studies suggest that reform of the non-discriminatory restrictions can yield between 75 and 90 percent of the total gains from reform (for example, OECD 2004). These results suggest that if Tunisia were to contemplate broader domestic regulatory reform initiatives aimed at non-discriminatory restrictions in sectors such as wholesale and retail trade, the gains could be several orders of magnitude greater than those projected here. The wholesale and retail trade, not included in this study, has a big potential for transforming the economy as the experience of many countries have shown.

Even when one sticks to a small number of sectors, the size of the gain for the economy depend on the extent of reform. To illustrate this, we compare a "full" reform scenario with "partial" one in the four chosen sectors. Here, full reform is defined to mean that all the discriminatory and non-discriminatory restrictions in telecommunications, banking and professional services are eliminated entirely, while air passenger transport is liberalized on a bilateral basis with the EU. So importantly, full reform would include reform of the non-discriminatory restrictions in the professions that appear to raise real resource costs. The welfare gains to the Tunisian economy from full reform are projected to be US $175 million per year after ten years (last row of Table E.3), compared to US $77 million per year from partial reform. And fully 80 per cent of the difference is accounted for by lower resource costs in the professions.

Box 3.5. Rent-Creating Versus Cost-Inflating Restrictions

The net effect of services liberalization on the economy depends on whether the restrictions to entry and business conduct in the different sectors are rent-generating or production cost-raising (Dee 2005). Rent-generating restrictions are akin to a tax, with the revenue flowing to incumbent firms rather than to the government. Removing these restrictions leads to an efficiency gain (the average number of efficient providers in the market increases) *plus* a rent redistribution among players in the market. Incumbent providers, whether domestic or foreign firms, tend to lose from this redistribution of rents while consumers and firm users of the service tend to gain. The *net* welfare gain to the economy can thus be small. When restrictions to entry and conduct increase the real cost of producing the service and/or doing business, liberalization is equivalent to a productivity improvement (saving of real resources). It increases the returns for the incumbent services providers and lowers the cost for users. The *net* result is thus a large gain for the economy as a whole.

Many studies of services trade reform simply assert whether barriers create rents or add to resource costs. For instance, the Konan and Maskus (2004) study of Tunisia simply assumed that services trade barriers were half rent-creating and half cost-escalating. Thus their projected gains in economic well-being from services trade liberalization were about 4 percent a year. But when they assumed the barriers to be entirely rent-creating, their projected gains fell to 0.33 percent.

Theory has provided some guidance. Rents are likely to be created by quantitative and other barriers that limit entry (or exit, though this is far less common). Some red-tape measures may add to resource costs. There are also many ways in which rents can be dissipated or capitalized. So, regulatory barriers that may once have been rent-creating for the initial incumbent can become cost-escalating for subsequent incumbents. For example, Kalirajan (2000) provides indirect evidence that some of the zoning and other restrictions common in the wholesale and retail sector create rents that are subsequently capitalized into the price of commercial land.

The limited empirical evidence from the second stage econometrics tends to accord with this intuition. In banking and telecommunications, where explicit barriers to entry are rife, barriers create rents. In distribution services, where indirect trade restrictions apply, barriers increase costs. In air passenger transport and the professions, barriers can potentially have both effects (Gregan and Johnson 1999; Kalirajan et al. 2000; Kalirajan 2000; Nguyen-Hong 2000; OECD 2005c; and Copenhagen Economics 2005). Barriers in maritime and electricity generation primarily affect costs (Steiner 2000; Clark, Dollar, and Micco 2004). Rents can be also dissipated or capitalized, so that regulatory barriers that were rent-creating for the initial incumbent become cost-inflating for subsequent incumbents. For example, Kalirajan (2000) provides indirect evidence that some of the zoning restrictions common in the wholesale and retail sector create rents that are subsequently capitalized into the price of commercial land. This study treats barriers on theory and available empirical evidence, rather than assumption.

How Would Tunisia's Firms Fare Compared to Foreign Firms

The reforms also have implications for the ownership structure of Tunisian industries. Surprisingly, even though many of the reforms remove discrimination against foreign suppliers, the projections do not suggest that domestically-owned services suppliers would be significantly smaller than otherwise (Table E.4). Only in the professions (the model's Other business services sector) are domestically owned firms projected to be smaller than otherwise—by less than 1 per cent, a result that could be easily absorbed by normal economic growth. In banking (the model's Other financial services sector) and communications, the domestically owned firms are projected to benefit from the removal of some of the discrimination against foreign firms.

One important reason for this is that domestically owned and foreign firms in these sectors have been modeled as providing closely, but not perfectly, substitutable services. In many services sectors, local firms in fact have local advantages that allow them to thrive alongside foreign providers.

Another reason is that, as in most other countries, the most intensive users of services are other services sectors, not agriculture or manufacturing. For example, there are typically more telephones in office buildings than in factories. So the sectors to benefit most from services sector reform are the services sectors themselves—not just banking and telecommunications, but also construction, trade and insurance. Most sectors in agriculture and manufacturing are projected to be slightly smaller than otherwise as a result of the services sector reforms. This is because there is assumed to be the same amount of skilled and unskilled labor available to the economy, whether or not the reforms take place. So if the reforms encourage some sectors to be larger than otherwise, then at least some other sectors need to be smaller than otherwise. But overall, the services sector reforms are good for the Tunisian labor market—real wages are projected to be 1.4 per cent higher than otherwise as a result of the reforms.

How Would Other Regions be affected by Reforms in Tunisia?

There are still some useful insights from the narrower set of reforms. Because the Tunisian reforms are mostly behind the border (with the main exception of the open skies agreement in air passenger transport, which is in any event bilateral), the gains to other regions from so-called "free-riding" are minimal. This has been observed in other studies of services trade reform. In the current case, the EU is in fact projected to lose slightly in welfare terms from unilateral reform of Tunisia's telecommunications and banking sectors. The EU is an important source of Tunisia's foreign investment in these sectors, so is adversely affected to a small degree by the loss of rents of its foreign multinationals in Tunisia. In other studies, trading partner countries can be slightly adversely affected by unilateral reforms, especially those that reduce costs in the reforming country. This is because such reforms improve the international competitiveness of the reforming country, so partners suffer a small terms of trade loss.

Reversing the argument, it means that Tunisia also has little to gain from behind-the-border reform in other countries. This is an additional reason why Tunisia should not wait for services trade reform initiatives to be reciprocated, except in sectors like air passenger transport where unilateral action would clearly be unwise.

How Would Reforms Affect Tunisia's Exports and Prospects of Diversification?

Appendix E confirms a significant boost in exports from the services sectors undergoing reform—by about 30 per cent in air passenger transport (including increased exports to foreign tourists), 50–70 per cent in communications, 10–20 per cent in banking and 30–50 per cent in professional services. Again, the export performance comes not just from the foreign-owned services suppliers in these industries, but also from Tunisian-owned firms, and contributes to a 0.9 per cent increase in total export volumes. The services exports shown in Table E.5 are those recorded in traditional balance of payments statistics—predominantly exports delivered via cross-border trade and consumption abroad (such as sales of services to foreign tourists). The growth in the output of foreign-owned firms in Tunisia (Appendix Table E.6), and the corresponding increases in their sales to other firms in Tunisia, represents an increase in Tunisian imports of services delivered via commercial presence. However, Table E.6 confirms that those same foreign-owned firms contribute significantly to increases in services exports delivered via other modes.

In summary, the services sector reforms examined here could provide small but useful benefits to the Tunisian economy. The economy is projected to be slightly bigger than otherwise, slightly more services intensive than otherwise, with a slightly bigger proportion of foreign ownership than otherwise, and with a greater export intensity than otherwise, providing a projected slight improvement in economic well-being.

Note that the representation of the Tunisian economy in the benchmark equilibrium in Table E.6 is after the injection into the FTAP model's database of the estimated initial barriers to services trade in each region (carried out using the GTAP model's 'altertax' procedure adapted to the FTAP model—see Malcolm 1998 for details), and after an increase in the relative size of the Tunisian communications industry, to better match national data (carried out via a taste shift in favor of communications). The benchmark equilibrium matches neither national data nor the GTAP model database exactly.

A further policy question is how the benefits from services sector reforms would compare to those from further reform of agriculture and manufacturing. This is the topic of the next chapter.

So it appears that on the basis of a rather restricted sample of services sectors, partial regulatory reform in those sectors would yield gains roughly equivalent to full unilateral reform of manufacturing tariffs, but roughly one tenth the gains from full bilateral reform of border protection in agriculture with the EU.

CHAPTER 4

Emerging Export Services

Where Does Tunisia Stand?

I n recent years, Tunisia has shown growing signs of real export potential in ICT and a
large number of professional services. The development of exports in these sectors can
help enlarge markets, realize economies of scale and create jobs. This chapter examines
what it takes to successfully compete in global market. It covers five sectors: ICT, accounting, engineering, legal services and health services.

The Potential and Opportunities

Trade in commercial services has grown considerably in recent years, such that services
accounted for 19 per cent of global exports in 2005. Services exports more than doubled
during the decade from 1995 to 2005, outpacing GDP as well as exports of agricultural
products and manufactures. Within the global services sector, professional and ICT-enabled
services are among the most dynamic growth segments.

The expansion of services trade has been driven by considerable reductions in communications, transport and transactions costs. Rapid advances in information and communication technologies and the ongoing global liberalization of trade and investment in
services have increased the tradability of many service activities and created new kinds
of tradable services. Many service sector activities are thus becoming increasingly inter-
nationalized, especially since advanced information and communications technology
enables the production of services to be increasingly location-independent. This development has led to the globalization of services activities, with associated changes in trade,
cross-border investment, and employment patterns (OECD 2006).

Moreover, demand for services has a high-income elasticity, so that services activities
tend to expand more than proportionally as countries grow richer. As a result, the services

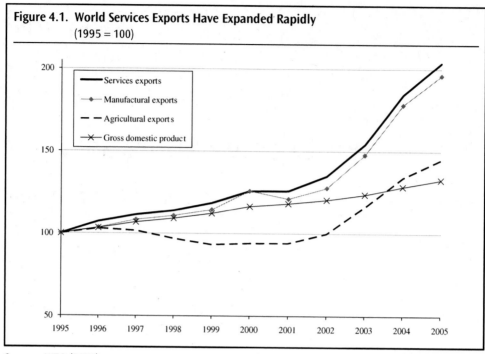

Figure 4.1. World Services Exports Have Expanded Rapidly
(1995 = 100)

Source: WTO (2006).

sectors in high-income countries are relatively bigger than those in middle-income economies, which in turn are more sizable than those in low-income countries. With the world economy projected to continue to grow at a strong pace, the prospects for service providers and services trade look bright.

Outsourcing Is a Major Driver of Trade

One development that has fuelled the growth of exports of professional and ICT-enabled services is the growing trend in high income countries for firms to outsource back office and information technology functions to take advantage of advanced skills and lower labor costs of specialized service providers. Most of the contracting-out is still undertaken with companies in the country of origin ("onshoring"), but cross-border arrangements ("offshoring") have been becoming increasingly common. Some observers predict that the value of offshoring activities to low wage locations will almost quintuple over the period from 2003 to 2008 (McKinsey Global Institute 2005a).

The aggregate potential for outsourcing to low wage locations has been estimated to reach more than 18 million jobs by 2008. Due to the limited need for direct client contact, regional knowledge, and complex interactions, IT services and packaged software are activities that are particularly amenable to being moved abroad. About 3 million jobs (44 percent of all ICT employment) could potentially be outsourced (McKinsey Global Institute 2005a). For some location-insensitive ICT-activities, such as call centers, the outsourcing rate could be even higher and reach more than 90 per cent.

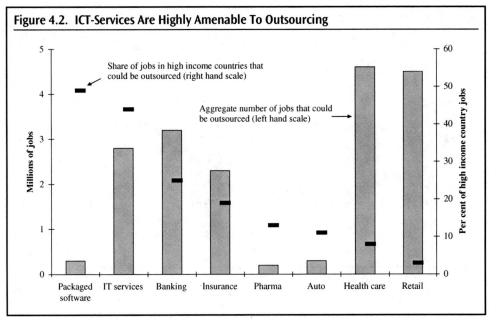

Figure 4.2. ICT-Services Are Highly Amenable To Outsourcing

Share of jobs in high income countries that
could be outsourced (right hand scale)

Aggregate number of jobs that could
be outsourced (left hand scale)

Millions of jobs

Per cent of high income country jobs

Packaged
software
IT services
Banking
Insurance
Pharma
Auto
Health care
Retail

Source: McKinsey Global Institute (2005a).

By 2003, about 7 per cent of ICT jobs in high-income countries had indeed been outsourced. The process is most advanced in the United States, the United Kingdom, and Germany. These three countries account for three-quarters of global outsourcing demand.

Offshoring for Francophone Markets Shows Significant Potential

In contrast, companies in francophone countries have been more timid to move employment abroad, and have limited their offshoring activities largely to call centers. Estimates indicate that more than 90 per cent of all back-office process outsourcing in French-speaking offshoring locations consisted of call centers in 2005, while in India the corresponding share amounted to less than 30 per cent (Roland Berger Strategy Consultants 2006). Despite this focus on call center offshoring, France shows a substantially lower call center intensity and outsourcing ratio than the United States or the United Kingdom. This low degree of outsourcing might partly reflect political and trade union resistance to moving employment abroad, but it could also suggest that France might experience an acceleration and catch-up in sourcing talent abroad in the medium-term future.

There are about 17,000 call center staff serving French speaking markets, of which more than three-quarters are located in Morocco and Tunisia. North Africa's wage advantage over Europe is not as pronounced as that of competitors in East Asia, but geographical and cultural proximity, well-established commercial ties, and the strong French-speaking communities make the Maghreb the destination of choice for "nearshoring" of French and other francophone companies. Outsourcing from the French market is projected to grow at an annual rate of 12–13 per cent over the next five years, i.e. at twice the rate of insourcing.

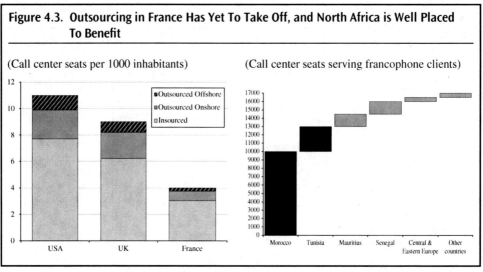

Figure 4.3. Outsourcing in France Has Yet To Take Off, and North Africa is Well Placed To Benefit

Source: Roland Berger Strategy Consultants (2006).

While companies in high income countries that outsource some of their services functions can realize cost reductions and thereby improve their international competitiveness, the receiving countries benefit through enhanced employment opportunities, including for women, increased FDI inflows, and improved service quality for the domestic market. In addition, there can be positive spillover effects through technology and knowledge transfer, and stronger incentives for individuals to invest in education. The prospects for growth in North Africa's emerging export services look good, but sectoral expansion is unlikely to create many jobs for the unskilled and poor, so that any poverty reduction aim would have to be realized through trickle-down effects of general economic growth.

Forward-Looking Policies Can Help To Grasp Opportunities

Tunisia has heavily invested in human and physical capital and undertaken important regulatory reforms in order to move the country towards becoming a knowledge economy. Many of these investments in, for example, telecommunication networks and higher education are now sunk and do not have to be considered any more when deciding on future-oriented governmental initiatives. What remains to be determined, though, is how public authorities can further improve the regulatory set-up and provide an enabling business environment in order for the private sector to take over the lead in propelling Tunisia in the desired direction of knowledge-based growth and prosperity.

The analysis in the following aims to contribute to the policy dialogue by describing and evaluating recent and prospective developments concerning professional and ICT-enabled services exports in the context of Tunisia's growth and competitiveness agenda. The discussion will thereby be comprehensive, covering health, accounting, engineering, and legal services, as well as software production, back-office processing, and call centers. The findings will be related to the performance of comparator countries in order to put them into a broader perspective.

The remainder of the chapter falls into three parts: First, Tunisia's recent performance in professional and ICT-enabled services will be discussed, with special attention to structural peculiarities of the sectors. Then, the international position of Tunisia's providers of emerging export services will be examined. Finally, a set of issues that warrant the attention of policy makers will be presented.

How has Tunisia Performed so Far?

Like many other services, professional and ICT-enabled services are important inputs to the economy. Provision of efficient services is essential to the overall country's competitiveness and productivity gains. At the same time, consumers should be protected against deceptive practices. The government has therefore to strike the right balance between opening/ liberalization (which encourages competition, cost effectiveness, and improved quality of service) and domestic regulation. The experience of Eastern and Central Europe shows that the opening of services sectors to foreign competition and the adoption of regional/ international standards can contribute to lowering prices and enhancing the variety and quality of services offered to local consumers. In a 2004 report on competition in the professional services sector, the European Commission found that outdated rules, including restrictions on advertising, recommended fee scales, and restrictions on entry into professions, resulted in seriously damaging anti-competitive practices and price-fixing.[79] While regulation is justified, flexibility is required to accommodate the evolution of the profession and the clients' needs.

Tunisia Is a Front Runner for Medical Services Exports in the Maghreb Region

Tunisia has a long tradition of exports in the health sector, in particular with its neighbor Libya. These flows have remained limited, however. With the emergence of so-called "medical tourism," prospects for trade growth are greater: while Tunisia was importing medical services from the North, patients now also come from sub-saharan Africa to benefit from cheaper surgery. Many countries have engaged in the race for attracting these patients, who spend more money in the country than regular tourists: fees paid to the surgeon, stay in five star hotels, excursions, and so forth. Tunisia is a front-runner in the Maghreb region, although a late-comer in the race by comparison with Asia or Latin America.

The two main Tunisian tour operators in the field are Esthetika Tour and Cosmetica Travel, both established in 2004, which attract each about 30 foreign patients a month. This activity therefore remains marginal. Beside tour operators (who just provide services ancillary to the surgical procedure: travel, transfers, hotel, excursions, and so forth), private clinics also attract foreign patients without any intermediary: these represent the bulk of patients, mostly coming from neighboring countries (80 percent from Libya). Finally, some tourists have to be treated for diseases/problems that occurred in the course of their stay in Tunisia.

---

79. Commission des Communautés Européennes, Rapport sur la concurrence dans les professions libérales, COM(2004) 83 final, 9 février 2004.

A recent study by the *Agence Française de Développement* (AFD) has made a significant effort to measure Tunisian exports of medical services.[80] Based on a survey of clinics, the study estimated that Tunisia hosted more than 42,000 foreign patients (2003), who generated an income of about DT 27 million for clinics (about 24 per cent of the clinics general output). Building on this estimate, the study evaluated the total amount of medical services exports to DT 69 million (including drugs and doctors' fees), and the general output for the Tunisian economy to DT 133 million (including accommodation and other expenses) and more than 10,000 jobs (of which half in the health sector).

Table 4.1. Libya Accounts for the Bulk of Tunisia's Medical Exports

	Libyans	Algerians	Europeans	Other Nationalities	Total
Number of foreign patients	34,034	1,320	4,484	2,373	42,211
Exports (DT million)	22.35	0.84	2.80	1.68	27.67
Exports/Total clinics' output	19.5	0.7	2.4	1.5	24.14

Note: based on a survey of 79 private clinics in Tunisia.
Source: Lautier (2005).

Engineering Exports Have Been Highly Successful

Tunisia counts about 12,000 engineers and 1,000 architects who are employed in both the public and private sectors. About 2,000 companies are specialized in the provision of design/engineering/consulting services. Among those, some companies have emerged as regional leading engineering firms, such as SCET Tunisia, STUDI and COMETE. For more than two decades, Tunisian engineering firms have exported their services—traditionally to other African countries, and now to the Middle-East and further. This early success resulted from the combination of several factors:

- foreign participation to the capital and technological transfers, including qualified personnel and know-how, which resulted in higher standards and reputation for quality;
- an initially largely protected domestic market, which enabled local firms to reach a critical size, gain experience, and then export;
- a voluntary donors' policy to short-list African engineering firms for projects in the region.

Engineering is the most open of all professional services sectors, and also the most successful on international markets. Major companies achieve double-digit growth rates, and trade takes place under all four modes of delivery.

---

80. Marc Lautier, *Les exportations de services de santé des pays en développement—Le cas tunisien,* Agence Française de Développement, Notes et Documents n°25, décembre 2005.

Accounting Trade Is Dominated By Large International Firms

Tunisia has 464 accountants (110 accounting firms) belonging to the Ordre des Experts Comptables, and 160 declared tax advisers, of which 40 belong to the Chambre Nationale des Conseils Fiscaux. The profession has grown rapidly, with a doubling of the number of accountants between 1997 and 2004. Access to the profession remains, however, very selective, with a little more than 30 students passing the exam each year out of more than one thousand candidates.

International trade is very important for the profession, although it primarily takes place through the business of the "big four," which are all represented in Tunisia (KPMG, Price Waterhouse Coopers, Ernst & Young, Deloitte & Touche). This illustrates the phenomenon of dualism of markets: the "big four" capture most of the trade generated by multinational companies operating in Tunisia. However, several caveats are needed: first, the Tunisian offices of the "big four" are entirely Tunisian (no foreign capital or foreign accountants), primarily by legal necessity (nationality requirements); second, the presence of these "foreign names" has been extremely beneficial to the profession in Tunisia, contributing to raising the standards and to training a number of accountants who could later launch successful individual high caliber practices; third, these firms employ a large number of accountants and staff (more than one hundred for the largest of them).

Trade in the sector takes place under all four modes of delivery: the majors have up to a third of their clientele abroad (Modes 1, through e-mail, and 4, through movement of accountants and staff abroad) and more than half of their clientele is made of foreigners (20 per cent of trade takes place under Mode 2). Mode 3 is the least developed of all modes, with only five Tunisian firms with offices abroad (in France). Trade is essential to the profession because of the limited size of the domestic market: expansion (or even survival) requires a look at export opportunities. Trade flows are not measured. Therefore, accounting is one of the most promising candidates for statistics improvement. First, accountants/auditors are required to declare some specific missions to the Ordre des Experts Comptables. This information could be collected to determine how much of the business is done with foreigners. Unfortunately, to date, firms have not diligently reported their missions. Second, the Ordre des Experts Comptables has recently started to offer to Tunisian accountants planning to travel for business a service of passport collection to obtain visas at the French Embassy. This information about visa requests would help determining the importance of Mode 4 for the profession; it would also help determining whether the profession is facing serious obstacles to mobility.

Finally, outsourcing might create new trade opportunities for Tunisian accountants and bookkeepers. So far, only three or four accounting firms are processing data for accountants based in France. These activities might expand in the future, due to technological progress and potential savings for French companies. However, obstacles remain, and new software applications already threaten the core activity of this trade (data processing).

Legal Services Remain Largely Focused on the Domestic Market

Tunisia counts about 5,000 lawyers, and the number of professionals is expected to double by 2012. This growth does not reflect, however, the good health of the profession—on the contrary, the Ordre National des Avocats suggested to reforming the conditions of access to the profession (creation of a new professional school) with a view to limit the flow of new entrants. The profession remains largely dominated by individual practices: only a dozen of specialized law firms emerged with significant international practice, up to 90 per cent of the practice with foreign clients (Modes 1 and 2). These Tunisian firms remain, however, very small, and they mostly serve as correspondents of major global law firms (Mode 1 exports) without being fully integrated. Only one law firm has offices abroad (Mode 3 exports).

The profession is strictly regulated and largely closed to foreign practitioners: only one foreign law firm could open an office in Tunisia, renouncing to the title of law firm and without the right for its lawyers (all Tunisian) to appear in court (the firm officially provides legal consultancy services only). About 80 per cent of this firm's legal consultancy services are supplied to foreign companies. This lack of openness did not prevent global law firms from doing business in Tunisia: as shown in Table 5, some major companies present in Tunisia sought legal advice abroad. Mode 1 became a substitute for establishment (Mode 3), increasing leakages in legal services trade.

ICT-Enabled Services Have Expanded Markedly Since the Late 1990s

The development of the ICT sector has been a major priority for Tunisia during the recent past, and the government has put down a number of ambitious performance objectives. In particular, the authorities have aimed to more than double the contribution of the ICT sector to GDP from 3.5 per cent in 2001 to 8 percent in 2006. Moreover, the presidential program for the period 2004 to 2009 reinforces the emphasis on ICT development by calling for the establishment of an appropriate base for a knowledge society.[81]

These objectives are achievable since the ICT-sector has been growing considerably in the recent past. Between 1997 and 2005, the number of ICT-firms almost tripled. The sector's contribution to GDP increased from 4.6 per cent in 2002 to 7 per cent in 2005, and employment grew from 40,200 to 55,200 over the same period. Export revenues surged from TUD 23.8 million in 2002 to TUD 51 million in 2005.

It should be noted, however, that most of the employment and revenues are generated by a few large public sector firms. Tunisie Telecom alone accounts for about two-thirds of sectoral revenues, and 40 per cent of the remaining revenues are estimated to accrue to other telecommunications and internet access providers (IDATE 2005). Thus, the almost 1 300 private sector IT enterprises, which had 10,115 employees in 2005, accounted for merely about 20 per cent of total sectoral output. Within the telecommunication sub-sector, the establishment of call centers has initially lagged developments in other Euro-Med countries, notably Morocco, but has quickly caught on. After the first two call centers were set up in 1999, the number of centers and related employment increased steadily. In 2005, 65 call centers were in operation, providing employment for 5,200 phone operators.

---

81. Several initiatives in the areas of infrastructure upgrading, human resource development, and regulatory reform have been pursued to meet the development objectives. Examples include major telecommunications reforms (for example, licensing of private mobile phone and internet access providers), institutional innovations (for example, establishment of the "Institut National des Télé-communications" and the "Agence Nationale des Fréquences"), and public promotion programs (for example, family computer program and internet connection of all schools). Moreover, Tunisia hosted the World Summit of the Information Society in 2005, which provided an international showcase for the country's achievements in the ICT-sector and its commitment for further development.

Table 4.2. Several Major Firms Are Trading International Legal Services

Tunisian law firms providing services to foreign clients (modes 1, 2, 3 and 4)

Law Firm	Size	Offices Abroad or Networks	Main Fields of Practice in Tunisia	Illustrative List of Clients and Deals in Tunisia
Abdelly & Associates	24 lawyers	Algiers, Tripoli	Corporate and M&A; banking and finance; oil, mining, and natural resources practice; telecoms and IT law.	Privatization of major oil company, development of a new airport, British Gas, Aurora Metals, Maghreb Minerals, SBC.
Adly Bellagha and Associates	7 lawyers		Corporate and M&A; banking and finance; arbitration; gas and oil.	Telecom Italia, Sterling Merchant Finance, City Bank, CIC, American Cooperative School of Tunis, Cementos de Portugal.
Cabinet Donia Hedda Hellouze	14 lawyers (5 partners)	Correspondent of important international law firms (France, UK, US).	Corporate and M&A; foreign investment; privatizations; banking and finance.	Privatization of cement plants for Secil, Colasem and Prasa, privatization of plaster plant Knauf, Telefonica.
El Ajeri & El Ajeri, International Consulting	15 lawyers (6 partners)	Correspondent of international law firms (France, United Arab mirates, Switzerland).	Corporate and M&A; banking and finance.	
Ferchiou & Associes Meziou Knani	41 lawyers		Corporate and M&A; privatizations; oil sector; commercial law.	Merrill Lynch, IBM, Orascom, Dubai Holding.
Kallel & Associates	7 lawyers (2 partners)	Affiliated with firms in Europe, the US and the Middle East. Tunisian representative of the *Alliance of Arab Lawyers*.	Corporate and M&A; energy; privatizations; intellectual property; arbitration.	Sale of country's cement producer and national energy generator.
Cabinet Malouche & Hamouda	8 lawyers (3 partners)	Affiliate of the World Services Group.	Corporate and M&A; communications; banking.	Barclays Bank, Banca di Roma, Club Med, Pepsi Co, Air France.
Mili and Associates	3 lawyers	Working relationships with international law firms (US, Jordan, Cyprus, UK, France).	Corporate and M&A; foreign investment; copyright law; competition law.	Price Waterhouse Coopers, Moore Stephens, Zeneca Pharmaceuticals, World Bank, Mitsui OSK Lines, Euro RSGC.

(continued)

Table 4.2. Several Major Firms Are Trading International Legal Services (*Continued*)

Law Firm	Size	Offices Abroad or Networks	Main Fields of Practice in Tunisia	Illustrative List of Clients and Deals in Tunisia
Salaheddine Caid Essebsi and Associates	7 lawyers (2 partners)		Corporate and M&A; banking and finance; arbitration; oil and gas sector.	
Zaaouni Law Firm	5 lawyers		Corporate and M&A; full practice.	
Foreign law firms established in Tunisia (mode 3—and ancillary modes 1, 2 and 4)				
Gide Loyrette Nouel Tunisie	11 lawyers (560 global)	French firm with 19 other offices around the world	Corporate and M&A; banking and finance; oil sector; electronics sector.	Santander and Attijari, major African and French banks, IFC, Merrill Lynch, British Gas, United Biscuits, Hilton.
Foreign law firms not established in Tunisia but providing legal advice to Tunisia-based clients (modes 1, 2 and 4)				
Herbert Smith LLP	1100 lawyers	UK firm with 20 offices around the world	Corporate and M&A; oil and gas.	British Gas, British Gas Tunisie, China National Petroleum Company, Senoc, other clients from China, India and Japan investing in Tunisia.
White & Case LLP	2695 lawyers	US firm with 37 offices around the world	Corporate and M&A.	Tunisiana.
Norton Rose LLP	1228 lawyers	20 offices around the world	Corporate and M&A; oil and gas; banking; aviation.	Nouvelair Tunisie, Calyon SA, Maghreb Minerals (acquisition of Tunisian zinc assets)

Source: based on Legal 500 and Martindale Hubbell.

Despite the marked growth of the ICT-sector, the overall employment effect remains limited. About 1.8 per cent of the economically active population works in the ICT sector. Hence, even a continuing strong expansion of the sector will only have a modest effect on bringing down the overall unemployment rate, even though it would certainly help to provide opportunities for currently underemployed graduates of technical schools and universities. Nevertheless, strong growth of ICT-jobs could make an indirect contribution to poverty reduction, as the value-added per ICT-employee is about four times as high as the national average, so that ICT expansion adds considerable purchasing power to the economy. The latter will tend to be partially exercised for the purchase of goods and services that are or could be produced by the poor and underemployed.

Most ICT firms in Tunisia are relatively young and small-sized. About 80 per cent of the companies have less than 50 employees. Yet, in comparison with high-income countries, Tunisia has fewer very small companies with less than 10 employees (Figure 4.4). This structural peculiarity might be due to the nascent stage of development of private sector demand for ICT-enabled services that does not support many "one man" companies targeting the supply of very specialized service products. Indeed, most demand for ICT-services in Tunisia comes from public sector enterprises that typically order larger scale service-packages.

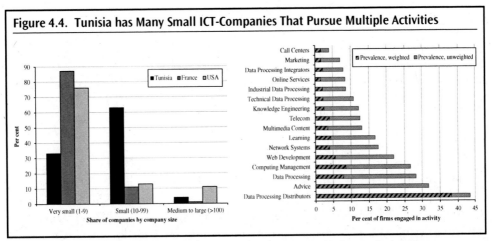

Figure 4.4. Tunisia has Many Small ICT-Companies That Pursue Multiple Activities

Source: IDATE (2005), McKinsey Global Institute (2005b), and Symboles Média (2005).

A related observation concerns the scope of activities that ICT-firms engage in. Analysis of 577 ICT companies listed in the most recent industry directory (Symboles Média 2005), revealed that almost half of all firms (and more than 70 per cent of all non-retail firms) pursued more than one ICT-service activity. Some companies engaged in as many as 13 different tasks. This broad scope of service activities might possibly be related to unstable domestic demand that makes a high degree of specialization undesirable.

The export success of Tunisia's ICT service providers has been mixed. While export receipts have increased in absolute terms, the country has been losing world market share in this very dynamic segment of international trade. Telecommunications and computer

& information services thereby show a somewhat differing picture. While export receipts from telecommunications services have firmly increased on the back of strong call center activity, so that the country's world market share rebounded from losses during the early 2000s, the corresponding share of receipts from computer and information service exports has merely stabilized at about half the level of five years earlier (Figure 4.5).

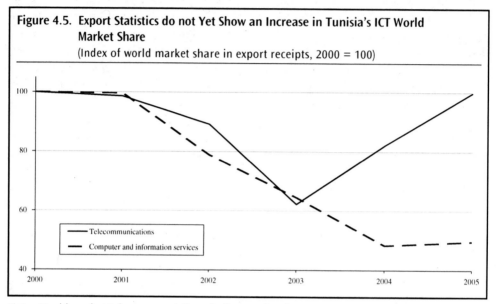

Figure 4.5. Export Statistics do not Yet Show an Increase in Tunisia's ICT World Market Share

(Index of world market share in export receipts, 2000 = 100)

Note: World market taken as consisting of all countries that report corresponding export statistics in all years from 2000 to 2005.
Source: WB staff based on IMF Balance of Payment Statistics, 2006.

The findings on the less than impressive export performance should be treated with care, as information on services trade is difficult to compile and the quality of statistics might not be as good as data on merchandise trade. However, the analysis highlights important diversity in the ICT services sector between the telecommunications and IT segments. Also, the strong headline statistics on the contribution of the sector to GDP and employment are apparently driven exclusively by dynamic developments in the domestic telecommunications sector, notably following the opening of the mobile phone market, and are not necessarily mirrored in international market success.

Is Tunisia Internationally Competitive?

Tunisia has a number of strength that would suggest potential for expansion of professional and ICT-enabled services. In the area of offshoring, locational attractiveness depends on several factors, including financial structure, people skills and availability, and the business environment. Some observers assign a higher importance to financial considerations (compensation costs, infrastructure costs, real estate costs, and regulatory costs) as the main

Figure 4.6. Offshoring Attractiveness Is Multidimensional

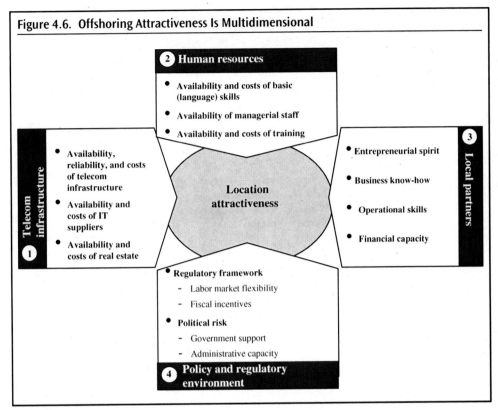

Source: McKinsey.

driver of offshoring decisions, but the other dimensions are similarly relevant (AT Kearney 2004 or McKinsey; See Figure 4.6).

Tunisia Has a Strong Human Resource Base

Tunisia produces generally a relatively large number of engineers and technicians, and according to the Ministry of Higher Education ("Ministère de l'Enseignement Supérieur"), the population of science and engineering graduates is scheduled to increase further. In particular, the cumulative number of scientists and engineers with higher education degrees is projected to more than double from 10,900 in 2003 to 22,600 in 2009. If this increase in graduates were to be achieved, the ratio of total science and engineering graduates to the population cohort of age 20–29 would increase from 0.6 per cent to 1.1 per cent.

In addition to requiring a high level of education and expertise, reputation is key in professional and ICT-enabled services. Tunisia scores well on this front also, and its most eminent doctors, engineers, accountants and lawyers often obtained a university degree abroad (in France, Canada, Belgium, or the United States). Exchange programs have been developed, for instance between French and Tunisian hospitals, and some joint degrees are put in place, for instance in accounting between the University of Lyon III and the universities of Tunis and Sousse. Some observers claim that about 9,000 Tunisian nationals

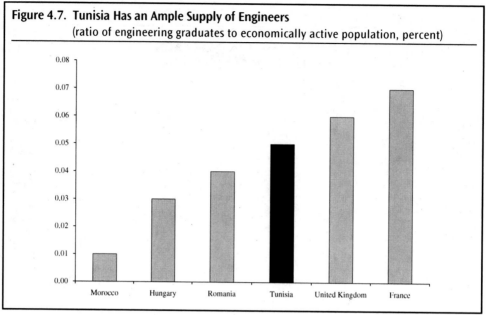

Figure 4.7. Tunisia Has an Ample Supply of Engineers
(ratio of engineering graduates to economically active population, percent)

Source: FIPA, 2006.

are now studying in France (13,000 around the world). Studies leading to professional services are particularly popular amongst these students: half of the scholarships granted to Tunisian students in France are in engineering sciences; similarly, about half of the doctoral students are registered in engineering.[82] This cross-fertilization contributed to harmonize the quality standards and to build networks across the Mediterranean. It also helps improving the reputation of the country.

Tunisian professional degrees are usually very selective. One can become accountant only after five years of specialized studies (and multiple exams) and three years of practical training. Tunisian doctors and engineers have an excellent reputation. The weak link is probably the qualification of lawyers, but a reform is underway. Similarly, in the health sector, reforms are underway to improve the quality of training of nurses and paramedical personnel.

Beyond the qualification of the professionals, standards are essential. In the accounting sector, Tunisia is one of the most advanced francophone countries, with Canada, in the implementation of IFRS standards—some lacunae remain, however, in the adoption of most recent updates or the presentation of accounts required by the Tunisian government. A Tunisian accounting firm even managed to obtain the PCAOB certification, which is required for auditing U.S. firms. The leading engineering firms are also ISO certified. Unfortunately, clinics have often neglected the adoption of international standards (their competitors in Asia are systematically ISO-certified)—a strategy to develop medical tourism will require to remedy this neglect.

---

82. Internet site of the French Embassy in Tunis.

Tunisia Appears Well Placed With Respect to Compensation Costs

Tunisia with its rich supply of well-trained technical graduates that are willing to work at moderate wages is in a relatively strong position as a services exporter. For example, the cost advantage of operating a call center in Tunisia rather than in France has been estimated to amount to 50–70 per cent. Tunisia thereby has a slight cost advantage over its main competitor, Morocco, and is only marginally more expensive as a location than Mauritius and Senegal, which tend to concentrate on providing less sophisticated services.

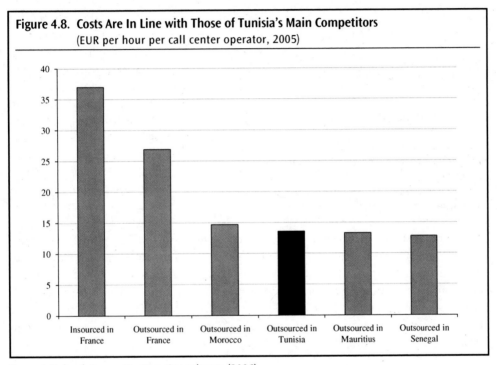

Figure 4.8.   Costs Are In Line with Those of Tunisia's Main Competitors
(EUR per hour per call center operator, 2005)

Source: Roland Berger Strategy Consultants (2006).

In industry surveys, low wage costs and the quality of human resources are frequently mentioned as a competitive advantage for Tunisian service providers, and the business environment is applauded by a tenth of all respondents in the ICT-sector (Figure 4.9). Also, Tunisia scores relatively well in rankings, such as the World Bank's Doing Business database or the World Economic Forum's competitiveness report, that evaluate the business environment and investment climate in international comparison. Hence many ingredients for success in developing new services exports and attracting offshoring business seem to be in place.

Tunisia's offer in professional services seems equally cost-competitive. For example, Tunisian companies can provide high quality engineering services at a lower price than their European competitors: according to the Association Nationale des Bureaux d'Etudes et d'Ingénieurs Conseils (ANBEIC), a Tunisian engineer is paid, on average, three times less than her European counterpart. Tunisian engineering firms are therefore

Figure 4.9. Industry Representatives See Strengths in Key Areas of Location Attractiveness
(Share of mention of particular issue as a strength of the country)

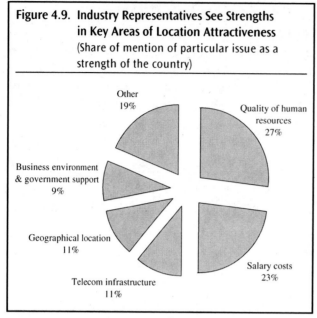

Note: Responses based on survey of 40 ICT-firms in Tunisia.
Source: Grupo Santander, Louis Lengrand & Associés, and Banque d'Affaires de Tunisie (2005t).

able to offer their services at half the price of European counterparts. If price prevails, however, and the technicality of the task is lower, some other developing countries (for example, China) appear to be even more competitive. This remark is valid for most professional services: Tunisia seems to have a comparative advantage in the provision of higher value-added services. Therefore, any sector development strategy should focus on reinforcing the quality pillar of Tunisia's competitiveness. The large supply of highly qualified personnel also helps keeping the wages relatively low compared to Europe.

A comparison of prices of the most common cosmetic surgery procedures around the world leads to the same conclusion: Tunisia is cheaper than Europe at large (including Central and Eastern Europe and Turkey), but it is more expensive than some Latin American and Asian countries. Within the region, Tunisia is also directly competing with Morocco. As a result, the country's attractiveness will mainly rest on the following factors: cultural (language and training of the doctors) and geographical (2.5 hour flight from Paris) proximity with Europe; and quality of the service provided (both medical and tourism components).

Lack of Scale Constitutes an Impediment for Conquering Foreign Markets

The small size of businesses is a general feature of professional services in the developing world. Tunisia is an extreme case, however, with a pre-dominance of family-owned businesses. This often results in management and marketing problems; also, access to credit (including export credits) is limited, due to the absence of physical guarantees of such small businesses—for the sector as a whole, credit is limited to 5 per cent of the firm's output, compared to 10 per cent in other sectors like tourism or manufacturing. This phenomenon affects all professional services:

- In the health sector, the number of beds per clinic is limited. As a result clinics cannot offer a complete range of services, and often do not have a critical size to become major exporters of medical services. This has to be contrasted, for instance, with private hospitals in Thailand, which are listed and can raise funds on the Stock Exchange.
- In the engineering sector, only three major firms emerged on international markets, with a relatively small size (hundreds of employees compared to thousands in

Figure 4.10. Tunisia's Offer For Plastic Surgery Procedures Is Attractive, But Not Lowest Cost

(US$)

	Rhinoplasty (nose reshaping)	Breast augmentation	Upper and lower eyelids	Facelift
US and Europe at large				
US	6,500 and up	6,500 and up	4,000 and up	8,000 to 12,000
UK	4,500 to 6,000	5,200 to 7,500	3,000 to 5,500	6,000 to 9,000
France	2,500 to 3,500	4,000	2,000 to 3,000	4,500 to 6,000
Germany	5,100	4,500	2,800	5,100 to 9,000
Spain	3,600	4,400	3,100	4,800
Belgium	2,400 to 4,200	3,000 to 5,000	2,400	2,400 to 4,500
Croatia	1,700 to 2,200	3,400	2,100	4,000
Czech Republic	2,700	3,500	1,800	3,000
Turkey	2,400	2,600	2,000	2,400
Africa				
South Africa	3,100	3,300	2,700	4,900
Egypt	2,200	3,000	1,800	3,100
Morocco	1,500	2,000	1,200	2,200 to 2,900
Tunisia	**1,800 to 1,900**	**2,300 to 2,600**	**1,400 to 1,800**	**2,700 to 3,600**
Latin America				
Brazil	2,300	3,500	2,300	3,000
Costa Rica	1,200	2,200	1,200	2,400
Asia				
India	1,300 to 2,400	2,000 to 3,900	1,500 to 1,800	2,700 to 4,200
Thailand	1,600 to 2,200	1,800 to 2,300	800 to 1,200	2,600 to 2,800
Philippines	800 to 1,800	2,000 to 3,300	1,300	1,300 to 2,400

Note: these prices were collected on websites of clinics offering plastic surgery procedures; they do not necessarily reflect the complete range of prices available; procedures can also vary, although an effort was made to chose the most similar procedures; price ranges can be justified either by the price-difference between clinics or by the price-difference between two more or less complex procedures or by the price-difference of for example implants (quality).
Source: diverse websites of private clinics.

major countries), and about 2000 micro-firms that could never reach a critical size to become significant exporters.
- In the accounting sector, only the "big four" have reached a critical size.
- In the legal sector, the number of specialized law firms is very limited (about a dozen) with a maximum of 40 lawyers. By comparison, the more open Morocco, could attract a dozen foreign law firms, each employing up to 250 lawyers.

In the ICT-sector, the government has made substantial efforts to promote computer and internet use by households and in the public sphere (for example, schools, government agencies). As a result, the information technology penetration has increased steadily, reaching 15 internet subscriptions and 50 computers per thousand inhabitants in 2005. Yet, in comparison with many medium income countries, the level of IT use remains low, and IT spending per capita is only a fraction of the spending in most OECD countries. In consequence, the private domestic market for information technology products is small.

With only modest private sector demand, ICT firms have the option of either supplying public sector organizations or searching for clients abroad. Many choose the former route, despite complaints about lengthy and cumbersome tendering procedures and poor payment morale of public agencies. Less than a third in a sample of companies reported that they realize more than 30 per cent of their revenues from exports, and less than 6 per cent claimed that they were oriented more towards the international than the national market (IDATE 2005).

The lack of export orientation can be partly attributed to the predominance of young, small firms that are short of overseas contacts, project references, and financial funds to acquire and execute international orders. Also, many of the start-ups are dominated by engineers who have their strengths on the technical and to a lesser extent on the marketing side of the business. Indeed, lack of information about overseas markets and shortage of marketing resources are cited by more than two-thirds of ICT-firms as important impediments to exports (Figure 4.11).

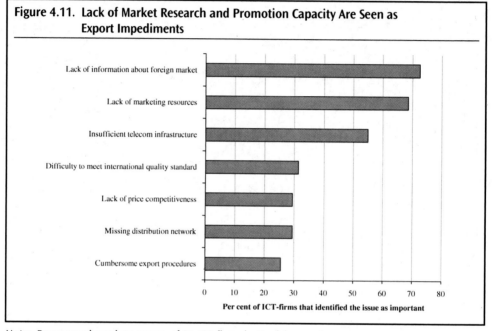

Figure 4.11. Lack of Market Research and Promotion Capacity Are Seen as Export Impediments

Note: Responses based on survey of 51 ICT-firms in Tunisia.
Source: IDATE (2005).

More than half of all interviewed firms also complain about an insufficient telecom infrastructure. Following major investments in the network and reforms of telecommunication regulation in the recent past (see Chapter 3), such a finding might appear peculiar. Yet, segments within the telecommunications sector remain that have not undergone any significant liberalization and the resulting monopolistic power of the incumbent service provider seems to result in low service quality. Indeed, when the World Bank team visited a call center operator in preparation of this study, the general manager reported that he had had a multi-hour phone service outage during the previous day. This was apparently not an isolated event, as the manager was quick to mention similar service cuts over the past year. He was furious about the lack of responsiveness of the telecom operator, who apparently had little interest in his complaints about income losses and reputational risk. He was even more upset about his own lack of provider alternatives, which forced him to stay put even when highly unsatisfied with the infrastructure service he was receiving.

How to Further Strengthen Competitiveness?

The preceding discussion suggests the existence of a number of opportunities and challenges to reinforce Tunisia's competitiveness and harness the benefits of deeper trade integration of professional and ICT-enabled services. One area of cross-cutting importance concerns the quantitative information about structures and developments in services trade that is available to policy makers. The quality of statistics on trade in services needs to be further improved, so as to enable the government to design suitable sectoral trade promotion strategies (including cooperation at the inter-ministerial level). International statistical guidelines and good practices are contained in the Manual on Statistics of International Trade in Services that has been developed and published jointly by six international organizations (UN, EC, IMF, OECD, UNCTAD, and WTO).[83]

Tunisia has multiple tools in hand to develop trade in professional and ICT-enabled services. Most progress could be achieved through unilateral reforms. Yet, bilateral agreements have proven very useful and a pragmatic approach to opening foreign markets: bilateral conventions on health, mutual recognition of diplomas or qualifications, facilitation of the movement of persons (visas). Regional negotiations could help promote a deeper integration of professional services within the Maghreb region and with Europe: beyond the removal of obstacles to trade, this level of negotiations facilitates harmonization of standards, practices, and regulatory frameworks. Tunisia could use the WTO to trade existing and prospective reforms for further market access with its major trading partners, and use international commitments to anchor domestic reforms, protect the government against future pressure of interest groups, and send a positive signal to foreign investors.

University Training and Professional Standards Can Be Reinforced

Quality is a main driver of professional and ICT-enabled services exports. Significant investments in education and standards improvement are therefore necessary to further develop trade. Professional and ICT-enabled services are amongst the high value-added activities that Tunisia could develop to diversify its exports and avoid falling into the trap of direct competition with low-paid and low-qualified workers in third developing countries.

The current professional education and training shows some shortcomings, though (World Bank 2007). A recent employment survey reveals a marked disequilibrium between supply and demand for certain professional qualifications. For some university degrees (management, finance, law), the number of graduates clearly exceeds the absorption capacity of the labor market, to the extent that more than two-thirds of all law graduates remain unemployed 18 months after finishing their studies. Hence, the universities need to find ways to improve the employability of their students and channel more of them into career paths with good employment prospects, such as engineering.

Moreover, the training of professionals should be adjusted to global markets' needs. In all sectors, interviewed firms complained about the loss of language skills—on top of Arabic, French should be preserved and English promoted. In the engineering sector, some specialties are insufficiently taught, and the profession regrets that schools train good tech-

---

83. UN document ST/ESA/STAT/SER.M/86 available on the websites of the six organizations.

nicians with no marketing skills. Some firms interviewed in the accounting sector deplored a decline in the quality of the young graduates.

In all professional services sectors, efforts are being made to reform training:

■ *Health:* In the medical sector, the quality of the doctors is often praised (local training is often supplemented by a specialization or an internship abroad), but lacunae remain for the training of nurses, midwives and other support or paramedical staff. In 2006, a reform was engaged for nurses, now recruited at the *baccalauréat* level and trained for three years in nursing schools (now university level). Programs were revised, but more efforts should be paid to learning languages if Tunisia wants to develop medical tourism activities. Similarly, paramedical disciplines (for example, thalassotherapists, nutritionists, physiotherapists) could be developed to meet the needs of health and well-being tourism.

■ *Engineering:* Training of the engineering profession was first reformed, in the late 1990s. Tunisian engineering schools have a good reputation, as illustrated by the existence of joint degrees with schools as prestigious as the *Ecole Nationale des Ponts et Chaussées* in Paris (Ecole Nationale d'Ingénieurs de Tunis). Exchanges exist at all levels, including research with other schools all around the world. Foreign firms do not hesitate to hire locally trained engineers.

■ *Accounting:* Access to the accounting profession is extremely selective in Tunisia: the small number of students passing the exam (3 percent of the candidates) and the length of studies and practice guarantees the quality of the professionals. Joint degrees have been developed with French universities, proving the high standard of the training. The rest of the profession is, however, less selective (bookkeeping and so forth).

■ *Legal services:* In May 2006, the Tunisian government adopted a new law regulating access to the profession of lawyer (*avocat*). The purpose was to create a professional school dedicated to the training of lawyers, and open to students with a law degree who successfully passed an entry examination. This reform would help containing the current stream of students accessing the profession without specialized knowledge and training, and controlling the quality and quantity of new lawyers. This reform was desirable. The profession has concerns, however, about the independence of the new school (and the profession), which is under the government's supervision—a lack of independence would be a serious drawback for the profession and trade. In addition, a four-year transition period was decided, which could create confusion and a challenge for controlling the flow of lawyers accessing the profession during this time.

Hence, the Government should maintain the pace of reforms in professional education so as to preserve the reputation of Tunisian qualified workforce and a high quality of service, adapt training to the global market's needs, and introduce international standards where possible (for example, promote the learning of foreign languages, improve the training of the nurses and medical support staff, internationalize the curriculum in legal studies, diversify the curriculum of engineers to include new disciplines and marketing), and introduce international standards where possible (for example, in clinics).

Restrictions to Market Access Can Be Reviewed

Liberalizing and opening professional services is not about suppressing domestic regulations: on the contrary, the maintenance of a high quality of service and the protection of consumers against malpractice are essential to the reputation and trade success of a country. Sometimes, liberalizing means adopting new rules. However, some rules are more restrictive than necessary to achieve legitimate policy objectives (such as the protection of consumers). In Tunisia, the interests of professionals seem to prevail over those of the consumers: the lack of openness limits competition on the domestic market, while the most efficient firms primarily supply their services abroad (duality of the market). Tunisian consumers and businesses would therefore be the main beneficiaries of the removal of unnecessary obstacles to trade in professional services.

Some obstacles are common to most professional services (for example, nationality requirements), but some others are more sector-specific. The table below attempts to benchmark professions using some elements of the restrictiveness index developed in Chapter 3. It shows that professional services are strictly regulated in Tunisia, and a census of all rules that might affect trade in each sector might be useful in the perspective of regional and multilateral negotiations: Morocco, for example, is a step ahead, and has completed this exercise in the lead-up to the free-trade agreement with the United States.

In the health sector, nationality requirements have a particularly negative impact on medical tourism. Many countries engaged in the competition attracted big names to promote their local practice (reputation). Tunisia excludes so far this possibility. One exception is for off-shore clinics but, as noted above, this formula did not seem to generate much interest in the investors' community, and it is probably not optimal from a development standpoint (limited positive externalities for the local population). Another exception is for training: foreign doctors can come to offer or receive training in Tunisia, with the authorization of the Ministry of Education and the Ordre des Médecins, but these movements are for non-profit purposes. These nationality requirements also largely defeat the purpose of agreements on the mutual recognition of diplomas. Otherwise, Tunisia suffers more from a lack rather than excess of rules on medical tourism: the government could take a new look at the corpus of rules to adjust it to the needs of this new form of trade and ensure respect of medical deontology and good practices.

Engineering is the most open of all professional services sectors—a common feature in many countries. Architecture remains more regulated. Nationality requirements are a problem, although companies could juggle with their counseling activities, and some foreigners have managerial positions in the leading Tunisian engineering firms. Diplomas are more easily recognized across borders. Some price controls exist (public buildings), but do not constitute a significant barrier to trade. The regulation that most affects trade in engineering services pertains to public tenders for construction projects (roads, railways, dams, and so forth). A recent reform raised concerns amongst the Tunisian engineering community due to the increased weight of prices in the selection process: some firms interviewed suggested that this regulation prevented new engineering firms to emerge and export after gaining enough experience on the domestic market; allegedly, the most reputable Tunisian firms could not compete for those markets anymore, because of the prices offered by foreign competitors. The 2002 regulation suggests that different rules are applied for "complex orders," but administrative burdens attached to these orders prevented any public body to qualify its order as such. Harmonization of these rules with the EU or other African countries could be useful.

In the accounting sector, strict nationality requirements also prevail: in order to become an accountant, a person needs to have been a Tunisian national for at least five years. This largely restricts establishment of foreign firms, although the "big four" could open offices entirely owned and staffed by Tunisians: part of a network, these firms use the name of a foreign company but remain fully Tunisian. Auditing is subject to a strict control of prices: the objective is to ensure that the cost of compliance with auditing requirements is not excessive for businesses. On the other hand, some firms interviewed suggested that the market could adequately regulate prices, and the current rules did not promote the improvement of the quality of the services offered. Some flexibility could be introduced to better take into account the difficulty of certain audits. Opening of the profession could also help promoting higher quality at a lower price.

Legal services are the most regulated of all professional services. De facto, it is impossible for foreign firms to practice law in Tunisia, and only one foreign law firm could open an office in Tunis (with great difficulties) with a practice limited to "legal counseling" (a profession that is not regulated). Barriers to trade also vary from profession to profession within the legal services sector: for example, the notary profession is even more heavily regulated than the lawyer profession. All usual barriers to trade are cumulatively used: nationality, residency, strict conditions on licensing, prohibitions on marketing, etc. The result is a closed sector that does not take off, despite signs of dynamism in more open neighboring countries. The specificity of national laws makes the opening of legal services always very tricky—however, the level of protection currently in place in Tunisia is unjustified in the light of legitimate objectives like the protection of consumers. In the current situation, it is impossible to tell whether the Tunisian market is just unattractive or whether barriers prevented any attempt of foreign firms to establish in Tunisia. Rules could be revised by the government in the light of new trade prospects.

In sum, obstacles to trade that are more restrictive than necessary to achieve legitimate policy objectives such as consumer's protection should be reviewed with a view to phasing them out. Possible examples of questionable regulatory measures concern the authorization of qualified foreign legal counsels to freely establish and practice in the country, the admission of qualified foreign doctors, and the authorization of private hospitals.

Structural Consolidation Should Be Encouraged

As mentioned earlier, one impediment to exports is the relatively small size of most professional services and ICT-firms with implications for the financial and managerial resources that are available for export promotion. Moreover, the lack of large offshoring companies means that Tunisian professional and ICT services have a low visibility overseas. In this context, a structural approach that balances a strong small and medium-sized enterprise sector with scale efficient national firms and affiliates of multinational companies seems to be called for.

The government has realized the size-related obstacles to the *ICT-sector's* development and has been trying to establish technology clusters in order to promote information exchange and business contacts. Providing equipped office space and financial incentives, such as three-year rental subsidies, five regional Cyberparcs (Gafsa, Le Kef, Moanstir, Siliana, and Kasserine) have been established to promote the creation of ICT-clusters within an office

Table 4.3. Numerous Restrictions on the Exercise of Professional Services Exist

Type of Restriction	Medical	Engineering, Architecture	Accounting, Auditing, Bookkeeping, and Taxation	Legal Services
Form of establishment	Clinic, hospital, individual practice	Bureau d'études or individual practice	Cabinet d'audit	Société d'avocats or individual practice
Foreign partnership/ association/ joint venture	Authorized, restrictions apply	Authorized, restrictions apply	Prohibited	Prohibited— exception for legal counsel
Investment and ownership by foreign professionals	Authorized, restrictions apply	Authorized, restrictions apply	Prohibited	Prohibited— exception for legal counsel
Investment and ownership by non-professional investors	Authorized, restrictions apply	Authorized, restrictions apply	Prohibited	Prohibited— exception for legal counsel
Nationality/ citizenship requirements	Must be Tunisian	Must be Tunisian	Tunisian for at least 5 years	Tunisian for at least 5 years
Residency and local presence	No	No	No	Must be a resident
Quotas/economic needs tests on the number of professionals and firms	Numerus clausus, e.g. pharmacy/ inhabitants	No, but for initial selection	No, but for initial selection	For some professions: e.g. notaries
Licensing and accreditation of foreign professionals	Possible recognition of foreign diplomas	Possible recognition of foreign diplomas	Possible recognition of foreign diplomas	Possible recognition of foreign diplomas
Licensing and accreditation of domestic professionals	Inscription on the Tableau de l'Ordre des médecins	Inscription on the Tableau de l'Ordre des architectes or ingénieurs	Inscription on the Tableau de la Compagnie des experts comptables	Inscription on the Tableau des avocats
Movement of people	Usual visa conditions, exceptional authorizations to practice (e.g. training)	Usual visa conditions, exceptional authorizations to practice (up to a year)	Usual visa conditions	Usual visa conditions, some bilateral reciprocity agreements
Activities reserved by law to the profession	Yes, practice of medicine	Yes, e.g. architect mandatory for most buildings	Yes, e.g. audit	Yes, e.g. notary acts, pleading in courts
Multidisciplinary practices	Authorized, restrictions apply	Authorized, restrictions apply	Authorized, restrictions apply	Prohibited, some exceptions

(*continued*)

Table 4.3. Numerous Restrictions on the Exercise of Professional Services Exist (*Continued*)

Type of Restriction	Medical	Engineering, Architecture	Accounting, Auditing, Bookkeeping, and Taxation	Legal Services
Advertising, marketing and solicitation	Prohibited for doctors, authorized for clinics with restrictions	Authorized, restrictions apply	Authorized, restrictions apply	Prohibited
Fee setting	Yes, distinction between public and private	For some activities only: e.g. public buildings	For auditing only	For some activities only: e.g. notaries

Note: This table does not pretend to be exhaustive: it gives an idea of potential regulatory obstacles to trade; the table also does not address the question of the adequateness of the domestic regulations: some are fully justified to ensure the quality of the service, and some might be more restrictive than necessary to achieve this end.
Source: Compilation of laws and regulations, restriction index based on Nguyen-Hong (2000).

Figure 4.12. Tunisia Needs A More Balanced ICT Size Structure

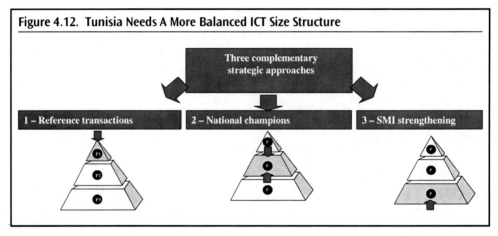

Source: McKinsey.

complex that can accommodate 50–80 technical employees each. By 2005, the five complexes together housed 48 ICT companies (software development, website maintenance, call centers) with a total staff of about 300.

In addition, the technology park El Gazala has been in operation since December 2001 on a surface of 65 hectares outside Tunis. This center serves as an incubator for newly-created enterprises, including advisory and financial support during the start-up phase, creation of an industry network and contacts with universities and international firms, organization of training and information exchanges, and management the common infrastructure and property. By 2005, El Gazala housed 38 companies, including affiliates of four multinationals (Alcatel, Ericsson, Huawei, ST Microelectronics). Total employment amounted to about 1000 people.

The ICT companies in El Gazala appear to be more export-oriented than the industry average, which might be partly due to the administrative and managerial support available as well as the greater opportunities for international contacts. More than a third of the companies installed in the technology park, employing half of all staff, work exclusively for export. A further sixth export at least a third of their output. Hence, further development of the Park could foster ICT-services exports and help to overcome the scale-disadvantage that many Tunisian firms face when trying to export.

In the professions, scaling up is a necessary step to international competitiveness: trade has to play a major role in the structural consolidation of the sector. The examples of the accounting and engineering sectors show that partnerships with foreign firms help to promote the sector's concentration and competitiveness. This, however, is not enough to ensure a long term growth of the sectors. Private sector's efforts should be relayed by coherent governmental policies. For example, in the *health sector,* the structural consolidation of the sector shall start at the government level: countries that are the most successful in the health tourism race, such as Thailand or India, have dedicated horizontal administrative structures that ensure the coherence of the strategies of the different ministries and actors. In Thailand, in 2004, the ministries of commerce and health collaborated to design a five-year strategic plan for medical tourism. An integrated approach would also ensure that key (and scarce) human resources are not diverted from the domestic market. The costs and benefits of an "off-shore" approach to health tourism could, for example, be balanced with alternatives such as the authorization of private hospitals open to both foreigners and locals (along the Asian model). Similarly, in the *legal sector,* the partial liberalization of trade could be an integral part of the legal and judicial reforms (including legal training).

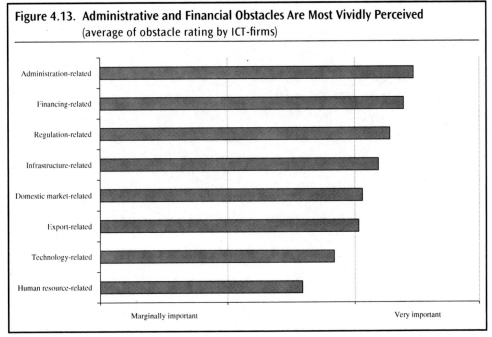

Figure 4.13. Administrative and Financial Obstacles Are Most Vividly Perceived
(average of obstacle rating by ICT-firms)

Source: Santander (2005).

Financing and Administrative Constraints Should Be Addressed

Due to their limited managerial resources, small-scale enterprises, such as professional and ICT firms in Tunisia, are particularly vulnerable to strict conditions for access to credit. Indeed, in the IEQ enterprise surveys, financing obstacles keep being mentioned as being of major importance for business and export development. Young university graduates might have a good business plan to launch a professional services or ICT-firm, but are held back by administrative requirements and lack of credit collateral.

The Government has set up SICAR risk capital schemes (Sociétés d'Investissement à Capital Risque), but the take-up by ICT-firms has been relatively low due to substantial collateral and guarantee requirements. At the same time, the Tunisian banking system is reluctant to grant credit to producers of immaterial services. Hence, pro-active efforts to strengthen the capital base of small-scale services firms and improve their access to credit appear called for to improve the business environment for professional and ICT-services firms.

Once businesses are set up, some administrative barriers prevail. One opportunity for government action concerns public tenders. Procedures are cumbersome, 40 percent of public tenders are later cancelled, and payments are often delayed for several months (Santander 2005). In this context, the Government should streamline tendering practices and adopt more timely payment schedules to free up scarce managerial resources and help to alleviate financial bottlenecks of small-scale services firms.

APPENDIXES

Definition of
Innovation Variables

Science and Engineering Enrollment Ratio, 2004 (as % of tertiary enrollment students) (UNESCO). This includes the fields of science (except social science), engineering, manufacturing and construction.

Researchers in R&D Per Million Population, 2004 (UNESCO). This is the total number of researchers engaged in R&D, as reported in the selected R&D indicators section of the UNESCO yearbook weighted by million population.

Total Expenditure for R&D as % of GDP, 2004 (UNESCO). Included are fundamental and applied research and experimental development work leading to new devices, products, and processes.

Scientific and Technical Journal Articles, 2003 (DDP). This refers to scientific and engineering articles published in the following fields: physics, biology, chemistry, mathematics, clinical medicine, biomedical research, engineering and technology, and earth and space sciences. National Science Foundation, Science and Engineering Indicators.

Availability of Venture Capital, 2006 (2006/7 WEF Global Competitiveness Report, Table 6.21). This is based on the statistical score on a 1–7 scale of a large sample group in a particular country responding to the question of whether entrepreneurs with innovative but risky projects can generally find venture capital in their country (1= not true, 7= true).

Patent Applications Granted by the USPTO, average for 2001–05 (USPTO). Shows the number of U.S. patent documents (utility patents, design patents, plant patents, reissue patents, defensive publications, and statutory invention registrations) granted.

Patent Applications Granted by the USPTO Per Million People, average for 2001–05 (USPTO). This is the variable above weighted by million population.

High-Technology Exports as % of Manufactured Exports, 2004 (DDP). High-technology exports are products with high R&D intensity, such as in aerospace, computers, pharmaceuticals, scientific instruments, and electrical machinery.

Private Sector Spending on R&D, 2006 (2006/7 WEF Global Competitiveness Report, Table 9.02). This is based on the statistical score on a 1–7 scale of a large sample group in a particular country responding to the question of whether companies spend heavily on research in their country (1= do not spend, 7 = spend heavily relative to international peers).

Firm-Level Technology Absorption, 2006 (2006/7 WEF Global Competitiveness Report, Table 7.02). This is based on the statistical score on a 1–7 scale of a large sample group in a particular country responding to the question of whether the companies in you country are (1= not able to absorb new technology, 7 = aggressive in absorbing new technology).

Value Chain Presence, 2006 (2006/7 WEF Global Competitiveness Report, Table 8.08). This is based on the statistical score on a 1–7 scale of a large sample group in a particular country responding to the question of whether exporting companies in your country are (1 = primarily involved in resource extraction or production, 7 = not only produce but also perform product design, marketing sales, logistics, and after-sales services).

Measuring Policy Restrictions in Services Markets

Services trade barriers are typically behind the border, non-price regulatory barriers, which may either: (i) protect incumbent service firms from any new competition, be it from domestic new entrants or foreigners; or (ii) discriminate explicitly against foreign operators. Governments use a range of restrictions to restrain services delivery. Some of them are natural, as in the presence of economies of scale or fixed costs for instance (for example, the number of services provider at a port container terminal is necessarily limited). Others are artificial, and stem from rules, regulations and norms that practically restrict entry into business. The barriers include exclusive or special producer and distribution rights for chosen providers, restrictive licensing (for example, banking, insurance), restrictive certification requirements (for example, in professional services), legislative discrimination against certain providers (such as nationality requirements, no application of the most-favored nation principle, etc.)–see Hoekman and Brago 1997 for more details. Many approaches to measuring restrictions exist, ranging from "shallow" assessments as in the GATS to more intrusive regulatory diagnostics such as in EU free-trade agreements (FTA) with its neighbors.

The GATS Approach to Measuring Restrictions to Services Delivery

GATS classifies restrictions in two main categories: (i) market access restrictions, which restrict the contestability of and entry into the markets without regard for the origin or nationality of the services or services provider and (ii) measures related to national treatment, which discriminate between domestic and foreign providers by limiting the access of foreign services and suppliers to domestic markets. When a WTO member binds a specific level of market access through GATS, it undertakes not to impose any new measures that would restrict entry into the market or the operation of the service, sending a signal of credibility to economic operators in other countries. WTO members are also required to disclose the "horizontal" legislations (those that apply to all sectors) that constitute barriers to trade in services, such as foreign exchange regulations.

Restrictions to services trade (market access and national treatment) are captured, under GATS, according to the mode of supply. Following a typology of trade in services developed by Sampson and Snape (1985), the GATS considers four modes of services delivery[84]:

- Firstly, some services are delivered in a "cross-border" fashion without either the supplier or buyer/consumer moving to the physical location of the other (mode 1 under the GATS language). Examples of this mode of services delivery include BPO such as call center services for customer service or medical transcription services ("other business services" in balance of payment statistics) which have registered rapid growth in recent years. Globally, cross-border trade accounted for 20 percent of global trade in goods and services in 2005 (Hoekman 2006). There is a strong link between services exports under mode 1 and commercial presence or FDI imports (mode 3, see below). For instance, in Tunisia's ICT sector where FDI are unrestricted, many foreign companies have entered the market to set up branches in order to export BPO services back to the parent or third-country client; Restricting export of services delivered through mode 1 (i.e., by telephone, Internet or electronic recording media) is very difficult, especially if the export market has a liberal telecom market as in the EU.
- The delivery of services may require the consumer may move to the producer's economy. In the language of the GATS, this mode of services trade is called "consumption abroad" or mode 2. Globally, this is the most widespread mode of services trade, with tourism and travel services largely dominating this category. Mode 2 is also the least restricted mode of services delivery: host countries often have no interest to do so (for example, promotion of tourism) while the consumer country's governments may find it difficult to restrict transactions under this mode, except for countries applying strict and effective foreign exchange restrictions, which is not the case of developed countries;
- Alternatively, the (firm) producer may move to the consumer's economy and provide the service via "commercial presence" such as when a foreign bank, telecommunications, or retailing firm establishes a branch or subsidiary in the territory of a country (mode 3)[85]. Commercial presence includes, inter alia, corporations, joint ventures, partnerships, representative offices and branches. Under this mode of services delivery, the host country's regulations regarding the establishment of a business and its activities are often the main obstacles (for example, FDI restrictions). While trade flows under the other modes of services delivery are captured more or less accurately by balance of payment statistics, those from com-

---

84. Services are not tangible and often not storable implying that its delivery often requires a local presence of suppliers even if information technology advances have made cross-border trade possible.

85. This has policy significance because it means that the GATS is a vehicle for negotiating foreign direct investment issues in the services area (mode 1).

mercial presence are not.[86] Available estimates put trade under mode 3 at 20 percent of global trade.

▣ Finally, the service provider may be a natural person who may need to move temporarily to the consumer's economy. In the language of the GATS, this mode of service delivery is called the "movement of natural persons" or mode 4. Services delivery under mode 4 can take two forms. It can be linked to commercial presence such as when employees of a foreign firm are temporarily transferred to a branch in the host country as intra-corporate transferees (for example, a foreign engineer temporarily transferred to a foreign branch from a parent construction *company*).[87] The second form of Mode 4 services provision, independent of commercial presence, involves professionals who are themselves services providers and need to travel to deliver services abroad. This second form is of high interest for developing countries endowed with abundant and well-trained workers. The host country's visa and labor market regulations constitute however a key factor in determining the prospect of expanding this type of export of services. With technological development however, there is a degree of substitutability between movement of natural persons and cross-border modes of supply in some sectors. Today, many computer and data processing services as well as accounting and even legal services can be supplied through cross border trade using the telecommunication infrastructure linked to the computer hardware, or simply through electronic recording media. However, for some sectors (for example, engineering and nursing), a natural presence is in the consumer's country is necessary.

The GATS framework acknowledges that a part from the explicit barriers to trade, governments' legitimate domestic laws and regulations aimed at remedying market failures or achieving legitimate social goals can obstruct trade. Indeed, Francois and Wooton (2000) have shown that the realization of gains from trade liberalization in services is closely tied to issues of market regulation and market structure. In many services sectors, market failures stemming from asymmetries of information or other sources abound and domestic regulation is needed to remedy information failures, market power abuses and to achieve social goals—Market forces alone may not deliver the most efficient or equitable outcomes. To protect consumers and users and to maintain high quality services, countries set standards for entry and conduct in some services sectors, such as in legal, health, and accounting. The legitimate regulations to overcome market imperfections often function as hidden barriers to trade, however. These domestic regulations are indeed often more restrictive than necessary for achieving their goals and incidentally or intentionally constitute barriers to entry and competition in the relevant sectors. They also are an impediment to international trade because of cross-country or cross-jurisdiction differences in technical standards, qualifications, and licensing requirements. Therefore, effective liberalization requires

---

86. There have been recent initiatives, especially by the OECD, to compile statistics on the activities of foreign affiliates (so-called FATS statistics). These and other statistics (for example, Karsenty 2002) suggest that reliance on balance of payments statistics alone can lead to an underestimate of services trade by more than 50 percent (Dee 2005).

87. The GATS requests WTO members to make commitments on the degree of restriction of the movements of high level staff, such as managers, executives and specialists.

governments to pursue regulatory and institutional reform inside the border—in addition to reducing explicit trade restrictions.[88]

However, GATS does not provide binding tools to deal with regulatory and institutional issues in WTO member countries. The classical GATS approach to "liberalization" consists of encouraging exchange of concessions between WTO members in order to come up with fewer explicit restrictions on the temporary movement of natural persons, commercial presence, cross-border electronic supply or capital movements. It only provides "guidance" in reforming behind-the-border barriers and "encourages" WTO members to design domestic regulations that do not distort trade. However, this guidance is not often followed in reality. The GATS approach is also very flexible in the sense that there is no binding constraint tying the extent and depth of the concessions made across modes (Box B.1). The flexibility in the GATS framework contrasts with the EU model of integration which may provide a better anchor for effectively ensuring that barriers to integration hidden in domestic regulation are identified and addressed.

Box B.1. General Obligations and Specific Commitments Under GATS

Under GATS, countries' liberalization commitments are grouped into two parts—the general obligations and the specific commitments. The general obligations include the MFN principle (Articles II and V), transparency obligations (Article III), and guidelines for dealing with non-tariff barriers (Articles VI through IX). Countries are bound by their general obligations for all services sectors, unless otherwise stipulated, which give all countries enormous flexibility. In contrast with general obligations, the market access and national treatment commitments that countries make in particular sectors and that included the separate country schedules for each mode, are legally binding. The market access commitment states that a country should allow the highest possible access to its market by not imposing certain types of quotas or quantitative restrictions.

The EU Approach to Integration in Services with Neighboring Countries[89]

The EU approach to trade integration in services within its broad neighborhood is based on a deep integration model, which aims at policy convergence as well as the liberalization of trade. Deep integration goes beyond the classical "liberalization" as undertaken

---

88. In situations of natural monopoly, sound government regulation is needed also to prevent abuse of market power and ensure good quality services. When capacity constraints in services supply (such as the size of the port) restrict the number of services providers, governments need to regulate to ensure that monopolistic suppliers or oligopolies do not abuse consumers and limit market access by charging prohibitive prices for access to the facilities/networks they control (Laffont 2005). The lack of sound regulation can indeed strongly undermines the quality of services in monopolistic situations. Adequate regulations and effective and independent regulatory agencies represent the best tool for preventing anti-competitive behaviors.

89. So far, only 3 Free Trade Agreements have been concluded outside the European Neighborhood. These are the FTA with Mexico, South Africa and Chile. Negotiations are currently ongoing with MERCOSUR, the Gulf Cooperation Council and the Africa-Caribbean-Pacific (ACP) countries. The first three seem to be mainly motivated by market access and competitiveness objectives while the ACP negotiation seems to driven by cooperation/ political/ and development objectives.

multilaterally through GATS. Deep integration implies some degree of regulatory convergence to reduce cross-country, cross-jurisdiction differences that affect market entry and conduct. In the EU model, the trading partner must adopt the EU acquis in the relevant services area in addition to eliminating the barriers to services trade in order to be part of the European Single Market. The objective is to come up with a common, fully integrated, market.

The EU model is particularly effective for countries joining the EU or participating to the EU Internal market. Free Trade Agreements have been concluded with countries that are Candidates to become EU members (Central and Eastern European Countries, Balkan Countries). Such FTAs include an important component of alignment with the EU *acquis* (deep integration). For these countries, the prospect of eventual EU membership is a fundamental premise underlying the policy convergence, which makes certain provisions and institutional arrangements, which might otherwise be objectionable, politically acceptable to the associated states.

For countries such as Tunisia for which Accession is not foreseen in the medium term, selective convergence towards specific features of the EU acquis is offered as part of the ENP. Many Mediterranean countries including Tunisia are in the process of negotiating the services component of their Association Agreements with the EU. It is expected that the future services agreements will include some degree of regulatory convergence in some sectors as stated in the ENP Action Plans adopted by these countries. The flexibility of the ENP means that Tunisia needs only to pursue convergence in the areas where it corresponds to the country's interests and level of development. For instance, for Tunisia to participate to the EU's common air aviation "skies," convergence to EU safety and security and other EU standards and norms is required. In other areas, mutual recognition of qualifications and accreditation (for example, for professional services provision) with some EU member States may be enough to ensure integration.

Thus, the ENP may allow countries like Tunisia to benefit from superior regulations (and to borrow import credibility) where it is relevant, making regulatory convergence consistent with improving institutional quality. The challenge is however to determine where gradual convergence makes economic sense and what would be the cost and the benefit to the economy, keeping in mind the country's development objectives and implementation capacity (Hoekman 2006b). The difference with Accession Countries is crucial to keep in mind. First, the incentive or "carrot" for reform may be seen as less attractive in the ENP since there is no membership to the EU in the near future. Second, without the attractive "carrot" of membership, any regulatory convergence will be scrutinized for suitability since regulations should be consistent with the local context.

The Approach Taken in this Report

The approach taken in this report goes beyond GATS but is less intrusive than the EU model of integration with Accession Countries. It measures restrictions based on "regulation" questionnaires developed by the OCED and the Productivity Commission of Australia that attempt to capture all the regulations that can affect significantly entry, competition and trade in services.[90] The questionnaires have been submitted to Tunisia's regulators, administration, and private sector in order to collect qualitative information on entry, competition and business conduct barriers in the following services sectors: banking, insurance, telecommunications, air transport, accounting, legal, and engineering services.

The approach consists of measuring restrictions based on "regulation" questionnaires developed by the OCED and the Productivity Commission of Australia that attempt to capture all the regulations that can affect significantly entry, competition and trade in services.[91] The questionnaires have been submitted to Tunisia's regulators, administration and private sector in order to collect qualitative information on entry, competition and business conduct barriers in the following services sectors: banking, insurance, telecommunications, air transport, accounting, legal, and engineering services.

The first step consists of collecting qualitative information about regulatory restrictions affecting services delivery in Tunisia and converting it into a quantitative index (or indexes), using weights that reflect the relative severity of the different restrictions. Clearly, some a priori judgment of the relative restrictiveness (i.e., the weighs of the restrictiveness index components) of different barriers is necessary and we use the general approach used by Findlay and Warren. The assignment of weights is generally less contentious within a given category of barrier than between them. For example, it makes sense to score a regime that restricts foreign ownership to 25 percent or less as being twice as restrictive as one that restricts foreign ownership to 50 percent or less. What is less obvious is how to weight the scores on foreign ownership restrictions together with those on licensing requirements, or those on restrictions on lines of business. Nevertheless, some of some of the inherent arbitrariness of the weighting procedures can be tested empirically.

One rich source of index measures, providing a benchmark reference, is the OECD studies of product market regulation (OECD 2005a, 2005b). We use OECD questionnaires to quantify the market entry and business restrictions in air passenger transport and the accounting, legal and engineering professions (see Appendix Tables E.2, E.4, and E.5). The benchmarking of Tunisia in these sectors is thus done against OECD countries. However, since the OECD questionnaires do not distinguish whether the restrictions affect only foreign operators or also affect domestic players, it is not sensible to use them for sectors such as banking where discriminatory restrictions are often rife. Here for banking and tele-

---

90. The first global project to capture restrictions in services was undertaken by the Productivity Commission of Australia. To date, this institution is one of the richest sources of database on services restrictions. Unfortunately, many emerging countries such as Morocco and Tunisia were not included in the project. The OECD is another source of regulatory restrictiveness. However, in terms of coverage, only OECD countries are included. There are some differences between these two sources, especially in terms of weight given to different factors of restrictions. For detailed discussion of the OECD methodology, see Conway et al. (2005) and OECD (2005a, 2005b). For a discussion of the Australia Productivity Commission methodology, see Dee (2005) and McGuire, Schuele and Smith (2000).

91. The first global project to capture restrictions in services was undertaken by the Productivity Commission of Australia. To date, this institution is one of the richest sources of database on services restrictions. Unfortunately, many emerging countries such as Morocco and Tunisia were not included in the project. The OECD is another source of regulatory restrictiveness. However, in terms of coverage, only OECD countries are included. There are some differences between these two sources, especially in terms of weight given to different factors of restrictions. For detailed discussion of the OECD methodology, see Conway et al. (2005) and OECD (2005a, 2005b). For a discussion of the Australia Productivity Commission methodology, see Dee (2005) and McGuire, Schuele and Smith (2000).

communication, we employ the restrictiveness index developed by Australian Productivity Commission (APC), which captures a measure of discrimination against foreigners—limitations on national treatment (see Appendix Tables E.1, E.3, and E.6). The APC restrictiveness indexes are also used for telecom because the OECD questionnaire gives too much weight to the share of the services providers in the market, whereas Tunisia's recent reforms are too new to induce the new providers to secure a large share in the market.

Once restrictiveness indices consistent with those generated by OECD and CAP are constructed for the different sectors, the second stage is to quantify the effects of these indexes of services trade barriers on some behind-the-border measure of economic performance—here prices or price-cost margins—while controlling for all the other factors that affect prices of services in that market. These econometric results are used to construct the counterfactual: what prices would be in the absence of the services trade restrictions, holding all other factors constant. The counterfactual comparison gives a behind-the-border 'tax equivalent', if the restrictions have raised price-cost margins, or a behind-the-border "productivity equivalent," if the restrictions have raised real resource costs. Studies along these lines include the OECD studies of product market regulation (OECD 2005a, 2005b; Conway, Janod, and Nicoletti 2005; Findlay and Warren 2000; Kalirajan 2000; Kalirajan and others 2000; McGuire, Schuele, and Smith 2000; Nguyen-Hong 2000; Doove and others 2001; Copenhagen Economics 2005; and OECD 2005c).

The FTAP Model—GTAP with Foreign Direct Investment

The FTAP model is a computable general equilibrium model incorporating services delivered via FDI. It was developed by Dee and Hanslow, (2001). It differs in turn from GTAP (Hertell, 1997), the 'plain vanilla' model from which it was derived, in three important respects.

First, because many services are delivered primarily via commercial presence, the modelling framework includes foreign direct investment as a mode of services trade delivery, and covers separately the production and trading activity of foreign multinationals. In other words, GTAP, the conventional multi-country model, is split out by ownership as well as location. In the current version of FTAP, the foreign ownership shares for Tunisia were obtained from survey data provided by INS. The relative size of the Tunisian communications industry was also adjusted upwards, compared with that in the original GTAP database, also based on value added shares provided by INS.

Second, by virtue of foreign ownership, at least some of the profits of foreign multinationals will be repatriated back to the home countries. Thus the profit streams in the conventional multi-country model have to be reallocated from the host to the home country, after provision is made for them to be taxed in either the home or host country. This reallocation leads to a distinction between GDP—the income *generated* in a region—and GNP—the income *received by residents* of a region. The latter forms the basis of (although is not identical to) the welfare measure in FTAP. The information on profit repatriation comes from the Balance of Payments Statistics of the IMF.

Finally, not all profits of foreign multinationals need be repatriated to the home country. Some may be reinvested in the host country. To account for this phenomenon, and to allow for the effect that regulatory reform may have on both domestic and foreign direct investment more generally, the model makes provision for savings and capital accumulation. This is particularly important, since some regulatory barriers are aimed directly at limiting foreign equity participation. It is therefore important to capture how regulatory reform will affect not just foreign ownership *shares*, but also the *total amount* of productivity capacity available to an economy. National savings rates are derived from the macroeconomic data in the International Financial Statistics and Balance of Payments Statistics of the IMF. Government savings rates are derived from the Government Finance Statistics of the IMF. Household savings rates are calculated as a residual.

The FTAP model also differs from GTAP in other respects. In particular, it allows for firm-level product differentiation. This is also important, since services tend to be highly specialised, being tailored to the needs of individual customers.

Source: Based on Dee and Hanslow (2001).

Questionnaires on Entry and Competition Barriers

TELECOM **Scoring Template (OECD Questionnaire)**			
Weights by Theme	**Question Weights[a]**	**Score**	**Question**
1/3			**ENTRY REGULATION**
	$w^t(1-w^m)$		What are the legal conditions of entry into the trunk telephony market?
		6	Franchised to 1 firm
		3	Franchised to 2 or more firms
		0	Free entry
	$(1-w^t)(1-w^m)$		What are the legal conditions of entry into the international market?
		6	Franchised to 1 firm
		3	Franchised to 2 or more firms
		0	Free entry
	w^m		What are the legal conditions of entry into the mobile market?
		6	Franchised to 1 firm
		3	Franchised to 2 or more firms
		0	Free entry
1/3			**PUBLIC OWNERSHIP**
	$(1-w^m)$		What percentage of shares in the public telecommunications operator is owned by the government?
			% government ownership/100*6
	w^m		What percentage of shares in the largest firm ion the mobile telecommunications market is owned by the government?
			% government ownership/100*6

(continued)

TELECOM Scoring Template (OECD Questionnaire) (*Continued*)

Weights by Theme	Question Weights[a]	Score	Question
1/3			**MARKET STRUCTURE**
	$w^t(1-w^m)$		**What is the market share of new entrants in the trunk telephony market?**
			6-normalized market share[b]
	$(1-w^t)(1-w^m)$		**What is the market share of new entrants in the international telephony market?**
			6-normalized market share[b]
	w^m		**What is the market share of new entrants in the mobile telephony market?**
			6-normalized market share[b]

[a]The weight w^m is the OECD-wide revenue share from mobile telephony in total revenue from trunk, international and mobile. The weight w^t is the OECD-wide revenue share of trunk in total revenue from trunk and international telephony.
[b]The market share of new entrants has been normalised to be between 0 and 6 with 6 being the smallest market share over all countries and 0 being the largest.
Source: OECD (2005b).

POSTAL SERVICES Scoring Template (OECD Questionnaire)

Weights by Theme	Question Weights[a]	Score	Question
1/2			**ENTRY REGULATION**
	1/3		**Do national, state or provincial laws or other regulations restrict the number of competitors allowed to operate a business in at least some markets in the sector: national post—basic letter services?**
		6	Yes, in all markets
		3	Yes, in some markets
		0	No, free entry in all markets
	1/3		**Do national, state or provincial laws or other regulations restrict the number of competitors allowed to operate a business in at least some markets in the sector: national post—basic parcel services?**
		6	Yes, in all markets
		3	Yes, in some markets
		0	No, free entry in all markets
	1/3		**Do national, state or provincial laws or other regulations restrict the number of competitors allowed to operate a business in at least some markets in the sector: courier activities other than national post?**
		6	Yes
		0	No

(*continued*)

POSTAL SERVICES Scoring Template (OECD Questionnaire) (*Continued*)

Weights by Theme	Question Weights[a]	Score	Question
1/2			**PUBLIC OWNERSHIP**
	1/3		**What percentage of shares in the largest firm in the sector: national post—basic letter services are owned by the government?**
		6	100%
		3	Between 0 and 100%
		0	None
	1/3		**What percentage of shares in the largest firm in the sector: national post—basic parcel services are owned by the government?**
		6	100%
		3	Between 0 and 100%
		0	None
	1/3		**What is the extent of public ownership in the courier activities (other than national post) sector?**
		6	Government controls all dominant firms in the sector
		3	Government controls at least 1 firm, but other firms operate as well
		0	No government involvement in the sector

Source: OECD (2005b).

BANKING Scoring Template (ACP Questionnaire)

Weight-Foreign Index	Weight-Domestic Index	Score	Restriction
			RESTRICTIONS ON COMMERCIAL PRESENCE
0.1900	0.1900		**Licensing**
		1.00	Issues no new banking licenses
		0.75	Issues up to 3 new banking licenses with only prudential restrictions
		0.50	Issues up to 6 new banking licenses with only prudential restrictions
		0.25	Issues up to 10 new banking licenses with only prudential restrictions
		0.00	Issues new banking licenses with only prudential restrictions
0.1900	0.1900		**Direct Investment**
			The score will be inversely proportional to maximum equity participation permitted in an existing domestic bank. For example, ownership to a maximum of 49 per cent of a bank would receive a score of 0.51.

(*continued*)

Weight-Foreign Index	Weight-Domestic Index	Score	Restriction
			BANKING Scoring Template (ACP Questionnaire) (Continued)
0.0950	0		**No New Licenses and JV Arrangements**
		1.00	Issues no new banking licenses and no entry is allowed through a joint venture with a domestic bank
		0.50	Bank entry is only through a joint venture with a domestic bank
		0.00	No requirement for a bank to enter through a joint venture with a domestic bank
0.0190	0		**Movement of People—Permanent**
		1.00	No entry of executives, senior managers or specialists
		0.80	Executives, specialists and/or senior managers can stay a period of up to 1 year
		0.60	Executives, specialists and/or senior managers can stay a period of up to 2 years
		0.40	Executives, specialists and/or senior managers can stay a period of up to 3 years
		0.20	Executives, specialists and/or senior managers can stay a period of up to 4 years
		0.00	Executives, specialists and/or senior managers can stay a period of more than 5 years
			OTHER RESTRICTIONS
0.1425	0.1425		**Raising Funds by Banks**
		1.00	Banks are unable to raise funds from domestic sources
		0.75	Banks are restricted from raising funds from domestic capital markets
		0.50	Banks are restricted in accepting deposits from the public, or face interest rate controls
		0.00	Banks can raise funds from any source with only prudential restrictions
			Lending Funds by Banks
0.1425	0.1425	1.00	Banks are not permitted to lend to domestic clients
		0.75	Banks are restricted to specified lending size or lending to Government projects
		0.5	Banks are restricted in providing certain lending services such as leasing, credit cards and consumer finance
		0.25	Banks are directed to lend to certain sectors such as housing and small business
		0.00	Banks can lend to any source with only prudential restrictions

(continued)

Weight-Foreign Index	Weight-Domestic Index	Score	Restriction
0.0950	0.0950		**Other Business of Banks—Insurance and Securities Services**
		1.00	Banks can only provide banking services
		0.50	Banks can provide banking services plus one other line of business—insurance or securities services
		0.00	Banks have no restrictions on conducting other lines of business
0.0475	0.0475		**Expanding Operations—Street Branches, Offices and ATMs**
		1.00	One banking outlet with no new banking outlets permitted
		0.75	Number of bank outlets is limited in number and location
		0.25	Expansion of banking outlets is subject to non-prudential regulatory approval
		0.00	No restrictions on banks expanding operations
0.0095	0		**Movement of People—Temporary**
		1.00	No temporary entry of executives, senior managers and/or specialists
		0.75	Temporary entry of executives, senior managers and/or specialists up to 30 days
		0.50	Temporary entry of executives, senior managers and/or specialists up to 60 days
		0.25	Temporary entry of executives, senior managers and/or specialists up to 90 days
		0.00	Temporary entry of executives, senior managers and/or specialists over 90 days
0*	0		**Movement of People—Board of Directors**
		1.00	Board cannot comprise of foreigners
		0.00	No restrictions on the composition of the board of directors
			The score is inversely related to the percentage of the Board which can comprise of foreigners. For example, if 20% of a BOD can comprise of foreigners they would receive a score of 0.80.
0.9310	**0.8075**		**TOTAL**

Table title: BANKING Scoring Template (ACP Questionnaire) (*Continued*)

*Weight was 0.019 in McGuire and Schuele (2000).

Source: Dee (2005a), based on McGuire and Schuele (2000).

Weights by Theme	Question Weights	Score	Question
— **OECD Questionnaire for Entry Regulations in the Professions**[a]			
2/5			**LICENSING**
	1		How many services does the profession have an exclusive or shared exclusive right to provide?
		6	More than 3
		4.5	3
		3	2
		1.5	1
		0	0
2/5			**EDUCATION REQUIREMENTS** *(only applies if licensing not 0)*
	1/3		What is the duration of special education/university/or other higher degree?
			Equals number of years of education (max of 6)
	1/3		What is the duration of compulsory practice necessary to become a full member of the profession?
			Equals number of years of compulsory practice (max of 6)
	1/3		Are there professional exams that must be passed to become a full member of the profession?
		6	Yes
		0	No
1/5			**QUOTAS AND ECONOMIC NEEDS TESTS**
	1		Is the number of foreign professionals/firms permitted to practice restricted by quotas or economic needs tests?
		6	Yes
		0	No

[a]The indicator for each profession is calculated as the simple average of the indicators of entry (Table 4) and conduct (Table 5) regulation.

Source: OECD (2005a).

OECD Questionnaire for Conduct Regulation in the Professions[a]

Weights by Theme	Question Weights	Score	Question
0.38			**REGULATIONS ON PRICES AND FEES**
	1		**Are the fees or prices that a profession charges regulated in any way (by government or self-regulated)?**
		6	Minimum prices on all services
		5	Minimum prices on some services
		4	Maximum prices on all services
		3	Maximum prices on some services
		2	Non-binding recommended prices on all services
		1	Non-binding recommended prices on some services
		0	No regulation
0.23			**REGULATIONS ON ADVERTISING**
	1		**Is advertising and marketing by the profession regulated in any way?**
		6	Advertising is prohibited
		3	Advertising is regulated
		0	No specific regulations
0.19			**REGULATIONS ON FORM OF BUSINESS**
	1		**Is the legal form of business restricted to a particular type?**
		6	Sole practitioner only
		5	Incorporation forbidden
		2	Partnership and some incorporation allowed
		0	No restrictions
0.19			**QUOTAS AND ECONOMIC NEEDS TESTS**
	1		**Is cooperation between professionals restricted?**
		6	Generally forbidden
		4.5	Only allowed with comparable professions
		3	Generally allowed
		0	All forms allowed

[a]The indicator for each profession is calculated as the simple average of the indicators of entry (Table 4) and conduct (Table 5) regulation.

Source: OECD (2005a).

AIR TRANSPORT Scoring Template (OECD Questionnaire)

Weights by Theme	Question Weights	Score	Question
1/2			**ENTRY REGULATION**
	1/2*w		**Does your country have an open skies agreement with the United States?**
		6	No
		0	Yes
	1/2*w		**Is your country participating in a regional agreement?**
		6	No
		0	Yes
	(1–w)		**Is the domestic aviation market in your country fully liberalized? That is, there are no restrictions on the number of (domestic) airlines that are allowed to operate on domestic routes?**
		6	No
		0	Yes
1/2			**PUBLIC OWNERSHIP**
	1		**What percentage of shares in the largest carrier (domestic and international traffic combined) are owned by national, state or provincial authorities?**
			% of shares owned by government/100*6

[a]The weight w is the average share of international traffic in total traffic (measured in '000 revenue passenger kilometres) for each country.
Source: OECD (2005b).

Modeling Result Tables

Table E.1. Direct Price Impacts of Tunisia's Regulatory Restrictions in Selected Services
(percent)

| | | Direct Price Impact | | |
| | | via markups on | | via Costs |
Sector		Output	Exports to Tunisia	
Currently				
Telecommunications	domestic providers[a]	6.8	. . .	. . .
	foreign providers[a]	15.5	. . .	. . .
Banking	domestic providers	7.5	. . .	. . .
	foreign providers	17.5	. . .	. . .
Professional Services	domestic providers[b]		. . .	6.0
	foreign providers[b]	19.1	19.1	. . .
After Unilateral Reform				
Telecommunications	domestic providers[a]	0.0	. . .	. . .
	foreign providers[a]	0.0	. . .	. . .
Banking	domestic providers	4.9	. . .	. . .
	foreign providers	6.8	. . .	. . .
Professional Services	domestic providers[b]			6.0
	foreign providers[b]	11.9	11.9	
After Further Bilateral Reform				
Professional Services	domestic providers[b]	. . .	. . .	6.0
	foreign providers[b]	6.4	6.4	. . .

[a]A simple average of price impacts for fixed line and cellular services.
[b]Simple average of estimates for legal, accounting, and engineering services.
Source: Dee (2005a), based on Warren (2000), Kalirajan and others (2000) and Nguyen-Hong (2000).

Table E.2. Sectoral Aggregation of the FTAP Model

Sectors in the FTAP Model	Corresponding GTAP Sectors
Live Animals, Products	Cattle, sheep goats, horses, animal products necessary, meat, meat products necessary
Dairy Products	Raw milk, dairy products
Coffee, etc, Sugar, Cut Flowers	Sugar cane, crops necessary, sugar
Fruit and vegetables	Vegetables
Cereals	Paddy rice, wheat, cereal grains, processed rice
Oil Seeds and Fats	Oil seeds, vegetable oils
Beverages and Tobacco	Beverages and tobacco
Other Agricultural Products	Plant-based fibers, wool, silk-worm cocoons, forestry, food products necessary
Fish and Products	Fishing
Mineral Products	Coal, oil, gas, minerals necessary
Metals, Products	Ferrous metals, metals necessary, metal products
Chemical etc	Petroleum, coal products, chemical, rubber, plastic products, mineral products necessary
Leather Products	Leather products
Wood Products, Pulp, Paper	Wood products, paper products, publishing
Textiles and Apparel	Textiles, wearing apparel
Transport Equipment	Motor vehicles and parts, transport equipment necessary
Other Machinery and Equipment	Machinery and equipment necessary
Electrical Machinery	Electronic equipment
Other Manufacturing	Manufactures necessary
Electricity	Electricity
Gas and Water	Gas manufacture, distribution, water
Construction	Construction
Trade	Trade
Other Transport	Sea transport, transport necessary
Air Transport	Air transport
Communications	Communication
Other Financial Services	Financial services necessary
Insurance	Insurance
Other Business Services	Business services necessary
Other Services	Recreation and other services, public admin, defense, health, education, ownership of dwellings

Source: Based on GTAP version 6 database.

Table E.3. Welfare Implications of Tunisian Unilateral and Bilateral Services Trade
Reform Initiatives
(US$ million)

Reform Scenario	Welfare in:			
	Tunisia	EU	GAFTA	Rest of World
Unilateral Telecommunications Reforms	21	−13	0	−1
Increased B2B Ecommerce	31	4	1	0
Unilateral Banking Reforms	3	−2	0	0
Unilateral and Bilateral reforms in the Professions	17	2	0	−5
Open Skies Agreement with the EU	4	14	−2	−37
TOTAL[a]	77	4	−1	−42
Full Reform in These Sectors	175	−18	−2	−42

[a]Individual entries may not add to total because of interaction effects.
Source: FTAP model projections.

Table E.4. Implications of Tunisian Unilateral and Bilateral Services Trade Reform
Initiatives for Sectoral Output in Tunisia
(percentage deviation from baseline)

Sector	Tunisian Firms Owned by:		
	Tunisia	EU	Rest of World
Live animals, products	−0.4	0.0	0.0
Dairy products	0.2	0.0	0.0
Coffee, etc, sugar, cut flowers	−0.6	−0.5	−0.5
Fruit and veg	−0.5	−0.4	−0.4
Cereals	−1.3	−1.2	−1.2
Oil seeds and fats	−0.9	0.0	0.0
Beverages and tobacco	−0.3	−0.2	−0.2
Other agricultural products	−1.3	−1.2	−1.2
Fish and products	0.0	0.0	0.0
Mineral products	−0.1	−0.1	−0.1
Metals, products	−1.3	−1.2	−1.2
Chemical etc	−0.9	−0.9	−0.9
Leather products	−0.8	−0.7	−0.7
Wood products, pulp, paper	−0.5	−0.4	−0.4
Textiles and apparel	−1.0	−0.9	−0.9
Transport equipment	−0.7	−0.6	−0.6
Other machinery and equipment	1.3	1.4	1.4
Electrical machinery	−0.8	−0.8	−0.8
Other manufacturing	−0.7	−0.6	−0.6
Electricity	−0.3	0.0	0.0

(continued)

Table E.4. Implications of Tunisian Unilateral and Bilateral Services Trade Reform Initiatives for Sectoral Output in Tunisia (*Continued*)
(percentage deviation from baseline)

Sector	Tunisian Firms Owned by:		
	Tunisia	EU	Rest of World
Gas and water	−0.5	0.0	0.0
Construction	0.1	0.2	0.2
Trade	0.3	0.4	0.5
Other transport	−1.1	−1.0	0.0
Air transport	16.1	16.6	16.6
Communications	1.2	10.4	10.4
Other financial services	0.5	7.0	7.0
Insurance	0.4	0.5	0.5
Other business services	−0.7	14.9	7.8
Other services	−1.4	−1.3	−1.3

Source: FTAP model projections.

Table E.5. Implications of Tunisian Unilateral and Bilateral Services Trade Reform Initiatives for Sectoral Export Volumes from Tunisia
(percentage deviation from baseline)

Sector	Exports from Tunisian Firms Owned by:		
	Tunisia	EU	Rest of World
Live Animals, Products	−5.6	0.0	0.0
Dairy Products	−1.3	0.0	0.0
Coffee, etc, Sugar, Cut Flowers	−1.5	−1.5	−1.5
Fruit and Vegetables	−3.9	−3.8	−3.8
Cereals	−2.6	−2.5	−2.5
Oil Seeds and Fats	−0.9	0.0	0.0
Beverages and Tobacco	−4.4	−4.3	−4.3
Other Agricultural Products	−1.7	−1.6	−1.6
Fish and Products	−2.3	−2.2	−2.2
Mineral Products	−0.1	0.0	0.0
Metals, Products	−1.8	−1.7	−1.7
Chemical etc.	−1.2	−1.1	−1.1
Leather Products	−1.0	−0.9	−0.9
Wood Products, Pulp, Paper	−1.2	−1.1	−1.1
Textiles and Apparel	−1.0	−0.9	−0.9
Transport Equipment	−1.1	−1.0	−1.0
Other Machinery and Equipment	1.3	1.4	1.4
Electrical Machinery	−1.2	−1.2	−1.2

(*continued*)

Table E.5. Implications of Tunisian Unilateral and Bilateral Services Trade Reform Initiatives for Sectoral Export Volumes from Tunisia (*Continued*)
(percentage deviation from baseline)

Sector	Exports from Tunisian Firms Owned by:		
	Tunisia	EU	Rest of World
Other Manufacturing	−1.1	−1.0	−1.0
Electricity	−3.9	0.0	0.0
Gas and water	−3.4	0.0	0.0
Construction	−3.3	−3.2	−3.2
Trade	2.3	2.4	2.4
Other Transport	−2.7	−2.6	0.0
Air Transport	28.3	28.8	28.8
Communications	58.6	73.1	73.2
Other Financial Services	11.7	18.9	18.9
Insurance	−0.9	−0.8	−0.8
Other Business Services	29.1	49.4	40.1
Other Services	−8.1	−8.0	−8.0

Source: FTAP model projections.

Table E.6. Structure of the Tunisian Economy Before and After Unilateral and Bilateral Services Trade Reforms

	In Benchmark Equilibrium	After Reforms
Output *(US$ million)*	37758	37811
Services share (%)	48.4	48.7
Value Added at Factor Cost *(US$ million)*	16335	16600
Services share (%)	67.0	67.5
Intermediate Usage *(US$ million)*	20439	20347
Services share (%)	34.0	33.9
Household Consumption *(US$ million)*	11611	11693
Services share (%)	37.8	37.8
Investment *(US$ million)*	5402	5421
Services share (%)	59.0	59.0
Government Consumption *(US$ million)*	3006	3027
Services share (%)	100.0	100.00
Imports CIF *(US$ million)*	10355	10438
Services share	10.6	10.9
Exports FOB *(US$ million)*	8976	9052
Services share (%)	25.0	26.2
Export Share of Output (%)	23.8	23.9
Foreign ownership share of output (%)	15.37	15.40

Source: FTAP model database and projections.

References

ACI (Airports Council International). 2004. *The Social and Economic Impact of Airports in Europe.* Airports Council International and York Aviation.

Agence Francaise de Developpement. 2006. *Evaluation du Programme de Mise à Niveau.*

Alavi, Hamid. 2004. "Good practice in trade facilitation: lessons from Tunisia." PREM Notes 89, The World Bank, Washington, D.C.

———. 2007. "Access to Pre-shipment Export Finance: Do Guarantees Help?" PREM Notes 113, The World Bank, Washington, D.C.

Anõs Casero, Paloma, and Aristomene Varoudakis. 2004. "Growth, Private Investment and the Cost of Doing Business in Tunisia." Middle East and North Africa Working Paper No. 34, Washington, D.C.

Arab Advisors Group, Strategic Research Service. 2005a. *Competition Levels in Arab Cellular Markets & Privatization Levels in Arab Cellular and Fixed Markets.*

———. 2005b. *Tunisie Telecom introduces the ADSL service for individuals and small businesses across the country.*

———. 2005c. *Tunisie Telecom's privatization progress.*

———. 2005d. *Upcoming Privatization of Tunisie Telecom.*

———. 2006a. *A Scorecard of Key Performance Indicators of Arab Telecom Operators.*

———. 2006b. *Cellular Rates in the Arab World: A Regional Comparison.*

———. 2006c. *WiMAX in the Arab World: Current status and regulations.*

AT Kearney. 2004. Making Offshore Decisions. Chicago.

Barry, Frank. 2003. "Economic Integration and Convergence Processes in the EU Cohesion Countries." *Journal of Common Market Studies* 41(5):897–921.

Barth, J., G. Caprio, and R. Levine. 2004. "Bank Regulation and Supervision: What Works Best?" *Journal of Financial Intermediation* 13:205–48.

Blomström, Magnus, and Ari Kokko. 2003. *The Economics of Foreign Direct Investment Incentives.* NBER Working Paper 9489. Cambridge, Mass.: National Bureau of Economic Research.

Boylaud, O., and G. Nicoletti. 2001. "Regulation, Market Structure and Performance in Telecommunications." *OECD Economic Studies* 32:99–142.

Buyck, Cathy. 2006. "Rising in the East." *Air Transport World* (May).

Clarke, George R. G., and Scott J. Wallsten. 2005. "Has the Internet increased trade? Evidence from Industrial and Developing Countries." World Bank Policy Research Paper 3215, The World Bank, Washington, DC.

Clark, X., D. Dollar, and A. Micco. 2004. "Port efficiency, maritime transport costs, and bilateral trade." *Journal of Development Economics* 75:417–50.

Conway, P., V. Janod, and G. Nicoletti. 2005. *Product Market Regulation in OECD Countries: 1998 to 2003.* ECO/WKP(2005)6. Paris: OECD.

Copenhagen Economics. 2005. "Economic Assessment of the Barriers to the Internal Market for Services." Copenhagen.

Dee, P. 2005. "A Compendium of Barriers to Services Trade." Prepared for World Bank. Available at http://www.crawford.anu.edu.au/pdf/Combined_report.pdf.

Dee, P., and K. Hanslow. 2001. "Multilateral liberalisation of services trade." In R. Stern, ed., *Services in the International Economy.* Ann Arbor: University of Michigan Press, pp. 117–39.

Dee, P., K. Hanslow, and T. Phamduc. 2003. "Measuring the cost of barriers to trade in services." In T. Ito and A. Krueger, eds., *Services Trade in the Asia-Pacific Region. NBER-East Asia Seminar on Economics, Volume 11.* Chicago: University of Chicago Press, pp. 11–43.

Diop, N. 2008. "On the Determinants of Private Investment in Tunisia." World Bank Policy Research Working Paper. Forthcoming.

Doove, S., O. Gabbitas, D. Nguyen-Hong, and J. Owen. 2001. *Price Effects of Regulation: International Air Passenger Transport, Telecommunications and Electricity Supply.* Productivity Commission Staff Research Paper. Canberra: Ausinfo.

EC. 2004. *A Community aviation policy towards its neighbors.* Brussels.

EC. 2006a. *Proposal for a Decision of the Council and the Representatives of the Governments of the Member States of the European Union, Meeting within the Council on the signature and provisional application of the Euro-Mediterranean Aviation Agreement between the European Community and its Member States, on the one hand, and the Kingdom of Morocco, on the other hand.* Brussels.

EC. 2006b. *Guide to Community Legislation in the Field of Aviation.* Directorate General Energy and Transport. Brussels.

Findlay, C., and T. Warren, eds. 2000. *Impediments to Trade in Services: Measurement and Policy Implications.* London and New York: Routledge.

Fink, C., A. Mattoo, and R. Rathindran. 2001. "Liberalizing Basic Telecommunications: The Asian Experience." World Bank Policy Research Working Paper No. 2718, The World Bank, Washington, D.C.

———. 2002. "An Assessment of Telecommunications Reform in Developing Countries." World Bank Policy Research Working Paper No. 2909, The World Bank, Washington, D.C.

Foreign Investment Promotion Agency (FIPA). 2006. *Tunisie: Une Economie Compétitive.* Tunis.

Freund, Caroline N., and Diana Weinhold. 2004. "The Effect of the Internet on International Trade." *Journal of International Economics* 62(1):171–89.

Gonenc, R., and G. Nicoletti. 2000. *Regulation, Market Structure and Performance in Air Passenger Transport.* Working Paper No. 254, ECO/WKP(2000)27, Economics Department. Paris: OECD.

Gregan, T., and M. Johnson. 1999. *Impacts of Competition Enhancing Air Services Agreements: a Network Modelling Approach.* Productivity Commission Staff Research Paper. Canberra: Ausinfo.

Grupo Santander, Louis Lengrand & Associés, and Banque d'Affaires de Tunisie. 2005. *Etude "Meilleures pratiques" sur l'Intégration du Secteur Privé dans les Chaînes Mondialisées de Production, de Distribution et d'Export dans le Domaine des TIC.* Final report to the l'Office National des Postes de la République Tunisienne. Tunis.

Guislain, Pierre, and Christine Zhen-Wei Qiang. 2006. "Foreign Direct Investment in Telecommunications in Developing Countries." In *2006 Information and Communications for Development, Global Trends and Policies.* Washington, D.C.: The World Bank.

Hanslow, K., T. Phamduc, and G. Verikios. 1999. "The structure of the FTAP model." Research Memorandum, Productivity Commission, Canberra, December, available from http://www.pc.gov.au/research/rm/ftap/index.html

Hertel, T. 1997, *Global Trade Analysis: Modelling and Applications.* Cambridge: Cambridge University Press.

Hertel, T., T. Walmsley, and K. Itakura. 2001. "Dynamic effects of the "new age" free trade agreement between Japan and Singapore." *Journal of Economic Integration* 16(4):446–84.

ICAO (International Civil Aviation Organization). 2004. *Database of the World's Air Services Agreements.* Doc 9511, CD-Rom.

IDATE. 2005. *Réalisation d'une Etude de Benchmarking Concernant la Compétitivité et le Développement des Entreprises Exerçant dans les Domaines des Technologies de l'Information et de la Communication.* Final report to the l'Office National des Postes de la République Tunisienne. Montpellier.

Institut d'Economie Quantitative. 2006a. *Evaluation du programme de Mise à Niveau.*

———. 2006b. *Rapport Annuel sur la Compétitivité 2006.*

InterVISTAS. 2006. *The Economic Impact of Air Service Liberalization.*

International Monetary Fund (IMF). 2006. Balance of Payment Statistics. Washington, D.C.

ITU (International Telecommunications Union). 2006. ICT Statistics Database. Available at http://www.itu.int/ITU-D/icteye/Indicators/Indicators.aspx.

Kalirajan, K. 2000, *Restrictions on Trade in Distribution Services.* Productivity Commission Staff Research Paper. Canberra: Ausinfo.

Kalirajan, K., G. McGuire, D. Nguyen-Hong, and M. Schuele. 2000. "The price impact of restrictions on banking services." In C. Findlay and T. Warren, eds., *Impediments to Trade in Services: Measurement and Policy Implications.* London and New York: Routledge, pp. 215–30.

Keck, Alexander, and Calvin Djiofack-Zebaze. 2006. "Telecommunications Services in Africa: The Impact of Multilateral Commitments and Unilateral Reform on Sector Performance and Economic Growth." World Trade Organization Working Paper, Draft.

Konan, D., and Maskus, K. 2004. "Quantifying the Impact of Services Liberalisation in a Developing Economy." World Bank Policy Research Working Paper 3193, Washington, D.C.

Lederman, Daniel. 2007. "Product Innovation by Incumbent Firms in Developing Economies: The Roles of Research and Development Expenditures, Trade Policy, and the Investment Climate." Policy Research Working Paper No 4319, The World Bank, Washington, D.C.

Lufthansa Consulting. 2006. African Aviation: Should government own their own airlines? (http://www.lhconsulting.com/fileadmin/downloads/studies/Airline_Privat_Africa.pdf).

Malcolm, G. 1998. "Adjusting Tax Rates in the GTAP Data Base." GTAP Technical Paper No. 12, Purdue University, West Lafayatte.

Mayer, J., A. Butkevicius, and A. Kadri, eds. 2002. *Dynamic Products in World Exports.* UNCTAD.

McGuire, G., and M. Schuele. 2000. "Restrictiveness of international trade in banking services." In C. Findlay and T. Warren, eds., *Impediments to Trade in Services, Measurement and Policy Implications.* London and New York: Routledge, pp. 201–214.

McKinsey Global Institute, 2005a. "The Emerging Global Labor Market: How Supply and Demand for Offshore Talent Meet." San Francisco.

———. 2005b. "The Emerging Global Labor Market: The Demand for Offshore Talent in IT Services." San Francisco.

Nabli, M., N. Bahlous, M. Bechri, M. El Abassi, R. El Ferktaji, and B. Talbi. 1999. "Trade, Finance and Competitiveness in Tunisia." In J. M. Fanelli and R. Medhora, eds., *Finance and Competitiveness in Developing Countries.* International Development Research Center.

Nguyen-Hong, D. 2000. *Restrictions on Trade in Professional Services.* Productivity Commission Staff Research Paper. Canberra: Ausinfo.

OECD (Organisation for Economic Co-operation and Development). 2004. *The Economy-wide Effects of Services Trade Barriers in Selected Developing Countries.* TD/TC/WP (2004)42. Paris.

———. 2005a. Indicators of Regulatory Conditions in the Professional Services. Accessed December 2 at http://www.oecd.org/document/24/0,2340,en_2649_37421_35858776_1_1_1_37421,00.html

———. 2005b. Indicators of Regulatory Conditions in Seven Non-manufacturing Sectors. Accessed December 2 at http://www.oecd.org/document/32/0,2340,en_2649_37421_35791136_1_1_1_37421,00.html.

———. 2005c. *Modal Estimates of Services Barriers.* TD/TC/WP (2005)36. Paris.

———. 2006. Potential Impact of International Sourcing on Different Occupations. Unclassified document DSTI/ICCP/IE(2006)1/FINAL. Paris.

Roland Berger Strategy Consultants. 2006. "Latest Trends in Call Center Offshoring in France." Paris.

Rossotto, Carlo Maria, Björn Wellenius, Anat Lewin, and Carlos R. Gomez. 2004. *Competition in International Voice Communications.* World Bank Working Paper No. 42. Washington, D.C.: The World Bank.

Rossotto, Carlo Maria, Khalid Sekkat, and Aristomene Varoudakis. 2003. "Opening up Telecommunications to Competition and MENA Integration on the World Economy." Middle East and North Africa Working Papers Series, No. 33, The Office of the Chief Economist, MENA Region, The World Bank, Washington, D.C.

Schware, R., and P. Kimberly. 1995. *Information Technology and National Trade Facilitation—Making the Most of Global Trade.* World Bank Technical Paper No. 316. Washington, D.C.: The World Bank.

Steiner, F. 2000. "Regulation, Industry Structure and Performance in the Electricity Supply Industry." Working Paper No. 238, ECO/WKP(2000)11, Economics Department, OECD, Paris.

Symboles Média, 2005. Les Technologies de l'Information et de la Communication en Tunisie. Business registry. Tunis.

Terrab, Mostafa, Alexandre Serot, and Carlo Maria Rossotto. 2004. "Meeting the Competitiveness Challenge in the Middle East and North Africa: The Role of Telecommunications Sector Reform." The World Bank, Washington, D.C.

Van der Mensbrugghe, D. 2005. "Prototype Model for a Single Country Real Computable General Equilibrium Model." Development Prospects Group, The World Bank. Processed.

Wallsten, S. J. 2001. "An Empirical Analysis of Telecom Competition, Privatization, and Regulation in Africa and Latin America." *Journal of Industrial Economics* 49:1–19.

World Bank. 2004. "Republic of Tunisia Development Policy Review: Making Deeper Trade Integration Work for Growth and Jobs." Report No. 29847-TN, Washington, D.C.

———. 2006a. "Textiles and Clothing: The Impact of the MFA Removal on Morocco, Tunisia, Egypt and Jordan." Washington, D.C.

———. 2006b. "Tunisia Agricultural Policy Review." Report N.35239-TN, Washington, D.C.

———. 2007a. *Doing Business 2008.* Washington, D.C.

———. 2007b. "Export Diversification in Egypt, Jordan, Lebanon, Morocco and Tunisia, Volume I & 2." Report N.40497-MNA.

———. 2007c. "République Tunisienne : Dynamique de L'Emploi et Adéquation de la Formation Parmi les Diplômes Universitaires." Washington, D.C.

Warren, T. 2000. "The impact on output of impediments to trade and investment in telecommunications services." In C. Findlay and T. Warren, eds. *Impediments to Trade in Services: Measurement and Policy Implications.* London and New York: Routledge, pp. 85–100.

Wells, Louis T., Jr., Nancy J. Allen, Jacques Morisset, and Neda Pirnia. 2001. "Using Tax Incentives to Compete for Foreign Investment. Are They Worth the Costs?" FIAS Occasional Paper 15.

WTO (World Trade Organization). 2006. *International Trade Statistics 2005.* Geneva.

———. 2005. "Trade Policy Review, Report by Secretariat, Tunisia." WT/TPR/S/152. Geneva.

Zhen-Wei Qiang, Christine, George R. Clarke, and Naomi Halewood. 2006. "The Role of ICT in Doing Business." In 2006 Information and Communications for Development. Washington, D.C.: The World Bank.